M000308752

Being Your Light

Messages from Gaia, Buddha, Jesus, Mary Magdalene, and Friends

Jill Renee Feeler

Being Your Light

Messages from Gaia, Buddha, Jesus, Mary Magdalene, and Friends

Jill Renee Feeler

Platinum Age Publishing
Boise Idaho

Being Your Light:
Messages from Gaia, Buddha, Jesus, Mary Magdalene, and Friends

© 2018 Jill Renee Feeler
All rights reserved

Platinum Age Publishing
Boise, Idaho

This book may not be reproduced, in whole or in part, without written permission from the author, except by a reviewer quoting brief passages, or a reader sharing on social media excerpts of fifty verbatim words or less and including a citation and link to the author's website. No part of this book may be stored in a retrieval system or transmitted in any form or by any means—electronic, mechanical, photocopying, recording, scanning, or otherwise—except in the author's Kindle version.

First Edition

Printed in the United States of America

Editor: Sonia Nordenson
Cover designer: Lathan Kaneswaran
Author photo: Raft Media

ISBN 978-0-9965315-1-1 (print)
ISBN 978-0-9965315-1-3 (ebook)

Author Website
www.JillReneeFeeler.com

Contents

Acknowledgments

This book is for everyOne who has the courage to know your capability, to claim the authority to be great, to trust that you can make God proud. Thank you. Cheers to you. And, please, carry on. Every pioneer of humanity has been where you are: pushing the envelope of what's possible here on Earth. Beyond the conventions of present human knowledge lies a frontier of wondrous discovery. It's for you that I do my work, whether you're a scientist, a rebel, an intellectual, a creative, a spiritual seeker, or simply a curious human.

I also thank my friends and family members, most of whom have little awareness of my work and may never even read this dedication. I love you, and I appreciate your respect for my unique ways of being me. I've always felt loved, and I believe that has allowed me to go this far out there in consciousness. To access timeless cosmic knowledge didn't feel brave, but destined.

Finally I thank the field of energy that I call my Team. Your respect and love for my own human authority has allowed me to take consciousness, spirituality, and sovereignty to new levels. I feel blessed to hold love, gratitude, understanding, sometimes anger, and mostly compassion for myself, and to offer the same to the human race from here in this bodysuit. It feels right that not waiting to die to "get it" is now possible. I pray for the leap forward for human evolution that we deserve, knowing how deeply loved and revered we are as a species of life, on a planet called Earth.

With God all things are possible. And so it is.

Introduction

Welcome. I'm so glad that you're here. You heard a call, didn't you? We each feel that desire to be part of something bigger than ourselves . . . something that is unprecedented—not just in our own lives but for all of humanity. And I am absolutely delighted that I get to be here alongside you, so to speak, in this process of you being your Light here and now.

For you the reader, this book could be quite a ride—a ride in which you have a lot of discretion and even control. Some may feel right at home in the moods, sensations, and ponderings of this material. And, because feeling at home here on Earth can be a rare thing, I'm honored to play any role in the love, comfort, self-respect, and personal value you can access here.

Others might have already noticed that, in writing the Acknowledgments, I used the word *God* twice.

You may now feel ready to run for the hills—to which I can relate on some levels of my own pragmatic and even intellectual self. Yet you may be pleasantly surprised by what is offered here for you.

I boldly assert that everything herein is offered to you *by* you—by an eternal essence of yourself that loves you, cares about you, and cheers you on . . . every single day and breath of your life. I can't prove that this is true, and wouldn't be silly enough to pretend that I can. I am a rationalist as much as I'm a spiritualist, and I feel blessed that I've been able to make enough room in myself for both of these qualities.

I've come to deeply appreciate that, just because something can't be proven, that doesn't mean it isn't real and true. I also assert that what might be true, even if it can't be proven, can lead to good for you and everyone when you believe it to be true. Please take a moment to let this in, as it's highly pertinent to the betterment of humanity in a way that science cannot assist.

Some truths based on faith or even hope are beneficial to the individual as well as the society, and I do wish that we all gave more consideration to areas of belief based on those factors. We are better humans when we know that we're loved by God, that we're forgiven when we mess up—even before we ask, and that we have far more potential for greatness than we typically give ourselves credit for.

Our betterment need not come at the expense of, or to the detriment of, any other. True betterment raises not just the bar of self.

It raises the potentiality of the entire human race, not in that they can do what the other did, although perhaps they can, but rather because one breaking free from a personal bondage of limited thinking and potential makes it easier for anyone (even everyone) to do the same.

I am also a pragmatic idealist, and I truly love the idea of a world where everyone knows herself or himself as individually special and loved, inherently beneficial, and capable of offering something of value to the community and to this world. Believing in oneself is an underrated aspect of personal achievement.

For me, the outer world in many ways routinely feels like the dystopia Ayn Rand described in her novel *Atlas Shrugged*. From a place within myself and yet beyond myself, I know that we're capable of more. Although this knowing isn't easy to articulate, I love words, and the challenge to express what I innately know about our capabilities is too tempting to ignore.

What you will receive or understand from my attempts here is beyond my control. All I can do is offer a way of knowing self—a knowledge that is far, far beyond the mind, and even beyond present-day notions of consciousness and enlightenment.

I didn't study such matters in school, courses, or books. I know from personal experience that at least some here on Earth have access to truths, to wisdom, that one would think requires decades of meditation, devoted study, apprenticeship to human masters, transformational near-death experiences, or even psychedelics. But that's not so in my case. I just know.

In many ways, I've always had knowings. There's a word for this: claircognizance. In around 2009 I began to more consciously acknowledge such knowings, which allowed me to more directly and easily will them into my accessible awareness and use them for intended good for myself, for others, planetarily, and even quite possibly beyond the scope of the planet.

I'm not a student of research, of science, of doctrine, or of consciousness and enlightenment. But I'm somehow a self-contained embodiment of some layers of knowing that are deep and philosophical yet readily applicable.

I've had no desire to study under other masters. That feels embarrassing to admit from a sense of its seeming arrogant, but it's nonetheless true. I humbly admit that I feel at one with such masters, for to me they are brethren, siblings, fellow masters here to share and offer as we all embody our individual versions of truth, light, love, and grace.

To directly address the notion of perceived arrogance, which I feel keeps many of my self-closeted fellow masters from acknowledging their own depth of knowing, my spiritual gifts and abilities don't make me feel better than others. Indeed, they make me feel more passionately dedicated to routinely offering what I know and what I "get" from my timeless-wisdom data-bank (I call it my God card) to everyone who is both interested and, I would hope, assisted by considering it for themselves.

My personal desire is not necessarily to dethrone any current teachings, especially if they're deemed as working well for an individual.

Do I feel that the principles I'm shown, and that I put to use, are better? Of course, or I wouldn't be deploying them for myself. But I greatly value free will and the authority for self that each of us humans has, whether we claim that and use it or not.

To be clear, my personal desire is to offer an upgraded set of truths, and of approaches for knowing oneself as being:

4

- gracefully forgiven (Earth life is often hard, and is by design a chaotic, unfair, and unpredictable experience)
- inherently valuable
- intrinsically flawed on the human level
- intrinsically flawless on the eternal/soulful level
- in authority over how one responds within one's human experience to the strange and surreal stimuli offered on Earth
- eternally sovereign
- the ultimate self-selector and initiator of one's human journey, which has been set in motion from a place eternal, quite conscious, and very much beyond this reality and the time-space continuum
- eternally loved

I receive feedback over and over again, from those who experience my work, about what an upgrade these truths, even individually, can mean for one's life. The level of freedom from suffering, acceptance of joy, and passionate pursuit of a better version of self for the sake of personal value and pleasure is in my view undeniable.

And that is more than worth the time and effort little old me puts into offering and sharing such concepts with this world. Part of me is always surprised that not everyone knows these truths, while other layers of me just gladly offer them, as a platform for healing, celebration, transformation, liberation, and moving forward authentically in one's life.

I do not desire students as much as I desire compatriots, each of us knowing ourselves as worthy, individual aspects of a loving, caring, and intelligent aspect of divine light, currently in human form in its naturally more limited state.

When I do come across doctrine, of pretty much any form or flavor, I find myself looking, superconsciously, for what is wrong with it, where it needs fixing, where it isn't yet working for the race of humanity, for this neck of the cosmos. It is analogous to a repair person called out to fix a broken air conditioner. They have specialized training in what to look for that's broken, that needs adjustment, tuning, and testing to set it right and have it in working order again.

Do I know that this sounds delusional and even recklessly grandiose? Of course. And yet, I know it as truth—not just in theory but in application, as I've put this cosmic tune-up skill set to the test in thousands of private sessions and hundreds of off-the-cuff public messages and stream-of-consciousness writings not unlike those in this book.

I somehow make room for this way of me being me along-side the also-very-real ways that I'm a wife to my awesome and very mainstream hubby of nearly twenty-five years and a mother to our two teenage daughters.

I'm also a parent to our fur babies and the caretaker of our household affairs, the holder of an MBA, a former strategic planning analyst in tech, and blah blah blah.

Accepting my soulful gifts and abilities doesn't mean I'm the most perfect version of humankind that one can achieve. The idea that in order to "reach" enlightenment one must correct all one's human flaws and failings was (and unfortunately still is) one of the greatest mistakes made in enlightenment teachings.

It didn't help that the Christian faith made Jesus into a flaw-less, sinless human, quickly making the pursuit of being that much in God's favor seem impossible for the rest of us. But that's not what Jesus would offer in his own account of his life story . . . Jesus readily offers to me that he could be quick to anger and was quite judgmental regarding what was right (i.e., good for the human and also for the collective) and what was wrong (i.e., self-destructive or at least not a contribution to one's lot in life, and possibly also detrimental to that individual's community).

Those who are new to my work, and curious, might wonder how I can say that Jesus is providing these additional insights to me, in real time. The answer? Because he is.

How do I know this corrected account of the story of Jesus that defies the doctrine and dogma? Could I take credit for everything that comes through me as being *from* me, as human Jill—because of something I read somewhere or learned through a sacred text, or something someone taught me, or something that just came to me?

Yes, I could, but it wouldn't be as real as the truth that the things I share are coming from a depth within me that is beyond this reality and beyond my humanness as Jill.

In the case of my spiritual connection, these divine revela-tions just happen to come with a clear sense of their being offered to me/us from beings we know from other times. Most often, I know them to come from a group of sacred energies who love and respect Earth and all of humanity, a group of higher-dimensional beings whom I call my Team.

These emissaries of Source consciousness sincerely care about the restoration of humanity's sovereignty. They don't want to become our authority figures, for they deeply respect our free will. They want all humans to know themselves as their own first point of authority with respect to their human journeys.

What I share is not stuff that I've been reading somewhere, have been taught, or have learned from my human journey. What I share is information that I am a creative vessel for, and that I choose to share. Do I know that it sounds ridiculous, and even crazy to some, for me to claim that something is from Jesus, Mary, or my Team? Yes, I do recognize this. Such claims would have seemed absolutely Looney Tunes to an earlier version of me, even as recently as ten years ago.

So I understand the criticism I sometimes face. But, being in the fortunate position of not needing my work to support me financially, I'm free to be real and authentic, no matter how "out there" the channeling of divine revelation might seem to some people.

And I'm in good company. After all, even Jesus was called crazy—as were Galileo, Van Gogh, Tesla, and many others who broke the molds of convention.

Whenever an author, inventor, composer, or scientist has a stroke of genius, a breakthrough idea, an aha moment, where do you think that comes from? It's something they didn't know before, and sometimes it's something no one had thought of before. What's the source, then?

In my view, it all comes from a divine will and curiosity that loves this reality, and that wants humanity to free itself from its own enslavement of limited thinking and suppressed creative potential. Even if the field of endeavor isn't "spiritual," it's all from Source. It's all God. Loving us.

I truly hope that you enjoy yourself in this information. I hope it inspires you, comforts you, stretches your current thinking, and makes you curious about what you can be, given the level of knowing now available for you.

In closing this introduction, one more thought. I observe that present-day science can prove what has already been created within the material planes to be stable, testable, and repeatable—for verification by those who desire to be responsible, respectable, and credible in this world. While credible is fine, incredible is even better in my values set.

I respect and honor the scientific process. I also respect and honor those who set thoughts, ideas, and creativity in motion in such a way that matter is changed by it, through individuals' actions, their beingness. Change that has been made real through matter sometimes attains levels never before experienced or even considered.

Scientific discovery, then, *follows* divine creation, animated through humans so curious about what's possible that they forget what's already known in order to test what can be. The science follows what has been created by divine energy. And when divine energy is conscious, it can be evolutionary.

Change agents on deck, in force, here, now. Lights up. Here we go!

With love, gratitude, and blessings,

Jill

Chapter One
A Spiral of Energy

As we get started, just relax your shoulders and take in some nice, deep breaths. Before you read on, I encourage you to close your eyes and start breathing in slowly through your nose and out through your mouth. That way, you'll center your energy right in that Light within yourself before we really get started with the "juice" of this book.

Beautiful. Please visualize within yourself a spiral of energy, like fireworks that have a corkscrew sort of effect. It's as if they're shooting up, and then there's this beautiful burst of energy.

That spiral corkscrew is actually starting in your root chakra, and you can imagine the spiral within you. Then visualize the fireworks bursting—first within your heart.

Next it'll soar up into the beautiful upper area of your brain and third eye and crown chakra. Another burst will happen there, and then you'll get the shower effect of those fireworks within your entire energy field, within the ball of energy in which you reside, within your humanness.

Imagine the sparks of Light flying . . . the sparks of your unique soul signature that no one else can be but you . . . the uniqueness that delights your Higher Self in ways we can't even imagine.

Relax those shoulders again, and please put a smile on your face. I have a message for you from all of our Higher Selves:

> We're happy you're here . . . so happy that you realize the power of your Light, the strength of your love, the meaningfulness of your compassion in your world on Earth. We want you to know that, by your being human, you change humanity, regardless of who else changes alongside you. As Jesus says, sometimes it only takes one.

Take a good, deep breath again, please. Sit up, letting your neck and spine get nice and tall.

Now each of your chakras will be spinning at what I'd call a platinum rate. The platinum frequencies are fully engaged within your major chakras, your minor chakras, and your other energy centers. Those platinum rays for this new era are surging and sorting. They're naturally pumping through your veins as if you were born to do this, because you were.

Beautiful. All right. You are allowing yourself to connect more fully with your soul signature through this experience. And now Archangel Metatron is sharing:

Metatron: Here You Are at the Top

> Well, that's enough priming the pump. Let's get started here. We're all very excited for this. We're at a new stage of the experience here. We were about to call it a game,

but we realize that, when it's called a game, that somehow dampens the relevance and profound nature of what's going on right here.

You might have been talking about the shift for quite a while; you've been building up to something, and feeling in some ways like you're a warrior in training. You've been figuring things out. You've been resolving yourself to align more fully with the Light that you are while you are also human.

You've debunked a lot of myths, you've plowed through a lot of nonsense, and here you are fully receiving that you are divine Light at the same time that you are human. And, while you've been doing all that, you've been uplifting the human grid system.

You have been building up to this time. What's interesting is that some were very excited about the buildup of the year 2012. There was a lot of chatter about the Mayan calendar at that time. And what we were doing also in that time frame of 2012 was helping you to feel the important role you play, helping you to feel like a bringer of energy into this reality—not just a receiver, not even just a carrier.

You brought your soul signature with you; you brought with you codes and activations and explosions of Light that would literally burn through anything within the human construct that didn't serve you as your soul signature and your Light.

You've been doing that . . . maybe without even knowing it. So you've been building up. You've been expanding, redefining, totally upgrading the human grid system by every single effort you've made to connect, to align with, to support, to nurture, to love, to shine your Light in this reality.

When we say you're at a top level with your spiral of energy, you made that spiral, you made those upper levels, and here you are at the top. It's as if you're at the top level of a stacked parking garage. Imagine that someone's looking for a high place from which to see the sunrise or sunset or catch the view. Let's just take a moment and catch the view of you, and of the upgrade you've allowed yourself to achieve relative to several years ago, maybe even several minutes ago.

Metatron: The View from Here

The view can be amazing from here. From this viewpoint you see beautiful things and you feel beautiful things. And you also have a better perspective for what isn't going in the way you would like it to. We're masterful enough that we don't need to deny that . . . we're not even going to ask you to not look, to pretend that's not there.

We're mature enough in our Light now to realize that, even when we're absolutely of rock-star quality in bringing in our Light and our soul signature, that doesn't mean that our relationships are what we want them to be.

It doesn't mean that our sense of feeling supported in this reality of Earth is what we want it to be. It doesn't mean that our health is what we want it to be.

Yet now we also realize that all of those challenges can be right alongside this truth that we are eternally Light, including now. That recognition that it all goes together is what actually allowed you to get to this top level. Our partner, Jill, is not liking those words "get to," as if that level was already there, because it wasn't.

That recognition that you are Light and you are human, and of all these situations that may not be what you want them to be—that seaming together of everything in your humanness and your eternal Light structure—is what allowed you to create the upper levels of this metaphor of the parking garage. It allowed you to have this view.

Chapter Two
The Production Crew
of This Reality

It's time to get down to brass tacks here. Because Jesus is saying, *Well, we've got to go to what's happening, Jill. Let's address what's happening.*

What's happening is that we've obviously gone through many a transition, but we've never done it from the level of humanness where you are right now. Just feel that for a moment. Humanity has never gone to the level of Light within its human grid system that it has reached right now.

So you noticed this. You noticed this as your Higher Self. All of you did, every single one of you who is participating right now by reading this book.

In the Galactic Council meetings in which we get to participate (usually while the body sleeps), where we discuss and review and laugh and console and giggle and strategize, we've reflected on this momentous level here, this view.

And we've realized that, from the view at this level, this expansion of Light is always present and available. It's available within a humanity that is connected with its full humanness, and fully accepting that not everything is perfect, yet still fully accepting its mastery.

We asked: *What could this offer us in terms of kind of pumping up this time on the planet even more?*

And what we as our Higher Selves started to consider is: *What if we, in our humanness, interacted with some of what normally goes on superconsciously with Gaia, and with other higher life forms?*

Higher doesn't mean above our Higher Selves. It's at the level of our Higher Selves, but there's a lot that goes on behind the scenes, like a production crew. In this reality, it's on-planet energy, it's off-planet energy, it's Pleiadian support structures, it's Andromedan support structures, it's everything—everything that loves and honors the Earth. And everything that happens on the Earth is part of this production crew.

And you know that we all have a Higher Self. So just imagine us all sitting around together, going, *Well, wait a minute, what if we invited our humans into this process?*

And there was this surge, this, like, *Whoa!*

Some said, *Can we handle it? Will we know what we're doing? Will we even have a clue how fantastic this is?*

And of course all of us as our Higher Selves said, *Hell yeah, we'll know, we'll show up, we'll know how amazing this is. We want to be a part of this seaming together of one human cycle into the next, the creating of the next great cycle.*

We want our human to be part of that, because our human is directly affected by it. Don't you see what we've been doing down there? We've

*been upgrading. We are much more savvy, much more wise to what's
really going on within our humanness, and we're making room for the
Light of Source that we are, no matter what's going on!*

So of course the other collaborators, all the other aspects of
the production crew, heard what we said, and they smiled and
said, *We get your point, let's invite them in.* And now here we are.

I would like you just to allow yourself to open to the recognition, to the confident feeling, that you are among the Higher
Selves, the Creator energy, that conceived of this reality. As
your Higher Self, you conceived of the concept of humanity and
every facet of physical and nonphysical energy in this world.

Gaia is right alongside you, delighted that the humans
showed up, ecstatic.

It's not a party until the humans show up, she just said. *Welcome.*

Can you feel that embrace from her? It's like every child-
hood dream of Mother Nature being right there next to you,
not looking down at you but looking at you eye to eye, with
nothing but love, honor, and respect . . . gratitude that you are
exactly who you are.

The Chamber of Light

Here's the way that I'm being shown this. You've been in this
kind of foyer of a Council meeting, and now these beautiful
crystalline doors with emerald handles are magically opening,
and you are naturally guided, ushered, into the chamber—the
Chamber of Light that oversees and helps support Light in
this reality.

And, as you walk in, you realize that there's a place for
everyone, a specially designated seat, something like the United

19

Nations, and there are names on all these seats, and microphones for translation if needed.

You realize that you are magically and magnetically drawn to a certain seat. It's like you're floating there, and as you sit down you see that you have everything you need: a notepad in case you want to write something down, a glass of Light for nourishment if you need it.

Also your name—your human birth name and every other name or nickname you have called yourself or been called, legally or unofficially—is somehow coded into a placard that's in your space.

It was ready for you. This space was created by you far into the future, with a hope and a dream that you'd be sitting here right now for this momentous occasion of the transition into a Platinum Age on Earth. And that's the miracle of linear time and the time-space continuum, both of which are pure genius.

You made it. It's like making a flight that you didn't know you were intending to take. Allow yourself energetically to just feel settled in to this position of authority, of Light.

There's a lot of attention on you, and on the other people who you see are there with you—a lot of kind of spectator gawking, as on a red carpet: *Oh, my gosh, they're here! They're here! The humans are showing up!* And it's said with pure joy.

Now you're actually receiving a standing ovation. The Pleiadians started it, and they're cheering out, *They see it, they see their Light! They know who they are now. Hallelujah and amen!*

And they're speaking other words of praise, in another language that I, as human Jill, don't know or need to know how to translate. You are bowing in gratitude, feeling the celebration for you and within you.

Interstellar Rock Stars

I just want you to relish this moment of your being one of the humans who are showing up for yourselves. You're no longer hoping for an outside force to rescue you.

You realized that you had a lot to work with, and stepped up to the plate of the human potential that was there all along, that we had all just forgotten.

And then you also realized, or were shown, or maybe are being notified only in this moment, that we are all bringing into humanity an upgrade that has never been here before.

So, yes, you're taking the original equipment and turning all the lights back on from the original-creation concept of humanity, which was interstellar rock star. And there is extra magic in your soul signature pockets from your packing for the trip of getting here.

You're all saying, *And we've got these! We've got a whole series, layers and layers, of upgrades that we've been adding to our humanity. We're continuing to add to it and will continuously be adding to it, bringing it online for humanity by humanity.*

Let's call this meeting to order, shall we? You're being invited to initiate, as the Chamber of Light is now in session. You call this meeting to order, and again there is applause erupting. I can hear your brain saying, *I don't know what's going on, but this feels amazing!*

My brain doesn't know what's going on, either, and I'm okay with that. I hope you are, too. It's just beyond the brain, and that's okay. Now we can relax a bit and join the other members of this Chamber of Light.

We're here to discuss and coordinate the seaming together of energy from this pinnacle of Light-based energies within humanity to this momentous time on Gaia, the planet Earth. Everyone's laughing at the mention of "this time"; it's a running joke in our Higher Self energy, because we can be nowhere other than in this time in the vibration. I just want to make sure you're in on that funny bit there.

Yet there is deep appreciation, obviously, for the time-space continuum in linear time as it functions, as it was designed . . . appreciation for the ingeniousness of it. It's amazing how this works here.

A Launch from the Pinnacle

It's been declared that this time will not be like previous times, that this time will bring a full launch from a pinnacle for all who choose to experience it as such.

My Team wishes to be clear that no one will be forced. No one will be imposed upon to propel themselves into this more expanded experience unless they choose it. No one will be forced. The regular practice of staying within the same parking structure platform will still be fully available to any who prefer that within their human consciousness.

We realize, they're saying, that you pioneers here, who are with us today, are again consistently pushing the envelope. You want more, and you deserve it. You will receive what you've asked for. You have the authority to ask for it, and our offering it to you is simply a formality. You are granted your wish of being connected fully and wholly to this highest level of Light, this pinnacle of Light that you've already received, already created from this point that you have attained.

And again there is applause, for many reasons. I ask my Team why, and they're just saying, *Many reasons . . . many reasons this is applause-worthy, Jill!*

Now you're being guided into a key visualization. It's very important for you, as one of the human ambassadors here, to visualize this; it helps greatly with this process for being your Light. I invite you to again close your eyes and relax your body, feeling fully connected as you did at the initial part of this conversation, when you were in the foyer connecting with your Light, feeling your majesty, trusting your sovereignty.

The Team and I would like you to again envision that spiral of Light that was within you. We'd like you to then imagine that you become like a paper doll, and then realize that you're magically unfolding in front of yourself into future versions of you, all stemming from where you are right now.

And as you imagine this natural unfolding and propelling forward of future "you's," you can imagine the corkscrew again. This time, the point of the corkscrew is coming from your heart space and the spiral is going in front of you, outwardly, still within your sphere, still within your ball of energy, but fully connecting you to all possible you's that are honoring of Light, honoring of the Light of God within you, honoring of the Light of God within all life, and providing upgrades aplenty.

Then just stay with me right here for a moment, as there will be a lot of energy really coinciding with the words that we just offered right there. You will have a lot going on, dear reader. If you have your legs crossed or arms crossed, just please uncross them for a moment, so you don't get tangled up, they're saying, in this energy.

Okay, good. And in this process you may feel the Light almost as if you're the heart, that organ of the heart, pumping. It's as if your human energy field, which is far bigger than your body and one hundred percent pure Light, is literally expanding, as if it's breathing, like a bellows. It's expanding as it breathes, and pumping your soul signature more fully into all of these future scenarios of you. You may feel exhausted, exhilarated, and energized all at the same time while this is going on.

Allow your own human to also receive this pumping of Light that is so very important. This should not be depleting your human energy field. It should actually be restoring and truly upgrading and transforming all facets of your present human today.

Nice!

Chapter Three
A Crystal Plasma You

And now, the next step. The Pleiadians will be guiding this one.

Please close your eyes and imagine again the paper doll scenario of future you's . . . so many you's. They go on forever, and every time you feel as if you've reached the end of the visualization of you's, you realize that there are more.

There is no end to these possible you's in this reality. They can all be glorious, and can have even more and more Light within each essence of you.

What we'd like you to notice next, though, is that it's as if there is a train track underneath all the you's.

This paper doll series, like a string theory, is coming forth from you, from your present you, you being the master, the master paper doll from whom these future you's emanate.

Underneath, you'll notice a radiant, plasma-looking Light grid, and it looks like a railroad track, and it just naturally appears. You are supporting it, rather than it supporting you. Your paper dolls, your future scenarios, don't need it.

You can call it a crystal you—a crystal plasma you. And beneath this crystal-plasma-you scenario is a natural support structure that looks like a railroad track. It's beautiful and translucent, almost like a neon light. You can't see the tube that's holding the neon light, but you know there is some structure there and it's glowing.

Jill here again. The color that I'm seeing is a beautiful purple-y indigo blue, what I call Pleiadian blue. You can have your grid, that railroad track, be any color you want.

Just feel those crystalline and plasma you's. They're naturally cascading out of you like a waterfall, but dancing in front of you, excited about you, excited about themselves, excited about the possibilities and feeling the support. You may even want to tap your feet a little bit, to indicate, *I feel that, I feel that railroad.*

Now, again, this part is very important. You don't need that railroad track; you burst forth and you can see these future you's without that. That railroad track structure showed up after you created those scenarios. So why is it there? If you don't need it, who is it there for?

That railroad structure is a hallmark of you and the other humans who make up this group. That hallmark is in many ways the same thing that helped you realize that you had a seat at this Chamber of Light gathering. It's the innate win-win/*If I move forward, I want everyone else to move forward* nature of you and your humanness.

I point this out because you probably feel it so naturally that you don't even realize that it's special, that it's unique, that it is a hallmark of you.

When you move forward in every part of you, you want everyone else to move forward with you. With every gain that you feel in your reality of Earth, you want everyone else to choose that gain.

Please, can this be offered to everybody? Can everybody move forward, please? You want to make sure of this.

You want to have a shiny railroad track there for anyone who starts to question the status quo. Anyone who is considering rebelling against the separation age, and anyone who gets a smile on their face at that idea of going rogue and going Light, and really starting to shine from within.

So it's that railroad track that you are laying down. You don't need it, but it's for anyone else who does. You want to make sure it's a little easier for them, that they can find it. That they can find that Light within them, choose that Light, access and declare and claim their sovereignty, and own their soul signature in this reality of Earth—even when it defies logic, even when it defies everything they've ever been told.

That railroad track is just so you. And the Pleiadians, from their perspective, are smiling, just beaming in agreement.

The Pleiadians: Process Successful

> *That is so you, and we love that about you. We love that—no matter how long this group decides to stay on*

27

Earth—you have laid tracks for all others, any other who seeks it out and chooses it and possibly goes through the same steps of expansion that you did, or maybe even creates their own.

The reason for this is so that, at some point, they can feel as if a hand has been reached out to them. And the message of that hand is, "Here, let me help you with that. I see that you're Light, too. I want to make it as easy as possible because I love you. I honor the fact that this is your effort and your upgrade, but if I can offer to shine any Light on the subject I will do that."

That will be you, leaving that track. So beautiful. Relax your shoulders please, pulling your neck up and away from your shoulder blades, making your neck nice and tall like a giraffe, rolling your shoulders a little bit, rotating your ankles gently, as the Pleiadians continue.

We've addressed what's going on here. We've addressed who you are and why you're here, from our perspective. We have successfully seamed your recent years with the upgraded pinnacle. Seam complete. Process successful.

As we say that, what we notice within each one of you is that your human spirit is like a rocket engaging with its booster.

We actually see it energetically right around your navel, in your belly button range.

There was this audible kind of "click" that we heard like a turbo booster within your lower chakras, with the Light launch of your upper chakras clicking firmly into place, including your soul signature with your humanness and everything that goes along with each.

They are fitting together seamlessly because you make it so, because you allow it to be your truth. Because you create fully from your humanness and fully from the Creator energy of your soul signature, of your eternal platform of Light that has always been and will always and forever be.

Jill: Becoming "God Goo"

And now there's a beautiful spiraling going on again. This time, there's a radiant beacon ball of light within your upper chakras. It's a big one.

It looks like a huge lightbulb, and it has a natural, spiraling dripping down of light, allowing the light to fully cascade into all facets of your humanness—every single layer: your physical body, your human relationships, your checkbook, your finances, your animals, your plants, your food.

Gaia has her own system, and she's gratefully receiving what you're offering as well.

The blessings of you, she just said, *are always gratefully, graciously received, with love and honor for all that you are.*

Now I notice that, with that light cascading down, there's also another beacon of light beneath the soles of your feet.

It's like a dyad, consisting of two elements. So there's one beautiful ball at your crown chakra, and one beautiful ball beneath your feet. Each one of them is ethereal . . . very other-worldly. And with the one beneath the soles of your feet, it would be like you're trying to balance on a ball, only you don't have to try. It's effortless, and you're just kind of rotating and pivoting on this ball that's beneath the soles of your feet.

That's helping you to carry your galactic, off-planet, omnipresent energy fields, helping you to carry the other end of your humanness from beneath the soles of your feet. It's helping us all to feel the otherworldly, supernatural, cosmically divine yet fully physical orientation of Light in this world.

Are you feeling a rotation in your body, as if your body is like a spinning top? It's very gently rotating. There's no need to stop that; you're literally resyncing, setting a new rhythm for your human energy field to fully embrace what you're doing, what you've done right here.

You might have a good spin going on. If you looked down at yourself from the ceiling, you might see yourself going counterclockwise.

Oh, how funny! They just said, *That's from the top, and on the bottom it's actually in a clockwise direction.* Wow, so just allow that to be felt in your physical body. Allow yourself to let the synchronization happen. This may continue a little bit throughout today and beyond.

Now I'm going to invite you, with your eyes open, to just kind of pump your fists a little bit, looking out from your human eyeballs and realizing that, yes, you just did this.

Yes, this just happened, and everything can keep changing in an upgraded fashion from here on, if you want it to. You don't need to wait for any outer events in order to experience this. Some of us are creating this life well before the full dawning of the Platinum Age.

So, whatever you're embracing, just let yourself declare right now that everything can start getting even better from here because you did that. Very beautiful. I encourage you to wiggle your toes, wiggle your fingers, and just tap your knees a little bit. Get back into your body by tapping your chin and touching your ears. Then a big body stretch here for me!

How are you doing? I have an image of some of you just being so like what I call God Goo! So "in it" that you might be saying, "I don't know where I am, and I don't know *what* I am right now." That's all right. You want to stay right there and not force it.

Accessing More of Your Soul Signature

I am so glad, dear reader, that you trusted. I know that every one of you is bringing something unique to the experience of reading this book. That Chamber of Light was obviously a place for each one of us; the guides made that clear. And I'm really applauding you that you came right along, even though you might be new to my work.

You trusted that you were meant to be here. With this work, we're just kind of scooping in everyone who feels drawn to it—for whatever they want to be, without holding back at all.

We're operating, as you can tell, at such a multidimensional level that our human receiving and processing of it all might require that we need to reread these messages multiple times.

Most of you will want to read through this more than once because of the miraculousness of it, in terms of the different parts of the energy being invoked and released and created at different levels within our humanness and within our Higher

Selves. As we reengage with it on our human level, it's very important and very relevant.

I'm confident that, for any of you reading this once and then reading it another time, especially at a later date, it'll be like, "Wow, I totally forgot about that part." It's so good that a book gives us that opportunity.

I'd like now to provide you with more information about that full launch from the pinnacle of Light-based energies within humanity. Our friends in the Chamber of Light are still hanging out with us, and they're saying, *Okay, are you going to show us what that means?*

So let's play with this, because we're going to be creating it as we go but, as Metatron is saying, *We can provide some information here.*

What my Team and I mean by this is, do you know that feeling of taking two steps forward and one step back, two steps forward and one step back? There has been a lot of that in these recent years, in the current age of humanity and of life on Earth. We make some forward progress, and then we take some steps back and it feels like we're right back where we started again.

Many of you have actually felt that in your life, how for many different waves or cycles of your personal life, it seemed like, "Yeah . . . I was doing so great, and then it was like what the heck happened, like I slid downhill for a while and then had to climb back up the mountain again."

It doesn't have to be that way, and one of the many reasons you readers are so unique and so clear in your lives is that, at various points along the way, you realized that some of the thinking and beliefs and energetic patterns and mental processes of Earth and humanity were not serving you.

Each of you reading this book—seriously, every single one of you—has at various points realized, "You know, that thought pattern, that energy pattern, that behavior pattern, is just not working for me. I'm going to have to figure out another way."

And the moment you did that, you began accessing more of your soul signature. What the Team and I can see is that many of you, especially in the last ten years or so, have realized that you actually do feel as if you're climbing the mountain without falling back again. Like you're getting more savvy at this being-your-Light thing while still in your humanness.

That is such a match for you showing up for an experience like this of reading these messages, doing the meditations and visualizations, and having your name on a spot predesignated for you by your Higher Self in that Chamber of Light.

Chapter Four
What Makes This a Platinum Age

This launch from the pinnacle is like a medal of honor or a graduation certificate. It indicates that you don't have to do the sliding-back part any more. Life doesn't have to feature so much of that two-steps-forward-one-step-back rate of progress. You might spiral around again regarding a certain issue, but you'll never be at the same level of the issue that you were before.

From now on, you will always be looking from an upgraded perspective. So, yes, to us the launch is a recognition, a validation. It's a giving yourself permission, meaning that you don't have to have that backsliding sort of experience so often any more . . . and some of you may choose never to have it again.

At a retreat that I led in Cancun, Mexico, a few years ago, we had a two-day workshop on the ancient Mayan wisdom. During that, the Team actually showed us really clearly that there have been other timelines on Earth, when many of us have been here, where we "raised the floor so that we could raise the ceiling."

In other words, if you imagine an elevator, the actual compartment that goes up and down, it was like the elevator did move up.

That can work, but there's another way to do it. I'm going to get really, really out there, so if your brain starts feeling bent into a pretzel, I apologize, but this is a part of progress for us here.

Here's what happens when you start to apply that elevator system across humanity. I know it doesn't seem this way, but in order for you to have your floor raised, you're basically pulling that lower option away from other people. If we start trying to raise our elevator car by taking away the third dimension from those who are still choosing it, we violate their free will.

Dear readers, that's how Atlantis imploded. The good guys did it, because we yanked away the third-dimensional lower-vibrational energies from those who were inhabiting that continent. And that didn't go well, as we know.

So what we're doing this time is what makes this a Platinum Age versus the reappearance of a previous Golden Age. (We've already been there and done that, right?)

To make it new, to make it a Platinum Age, we're actually leaving the floor exactly where it is. That makes it more challenging, because that lower-vibrational feeling is still available for any of us to have.

Whatever that lower-vibe feeling is for you! Stress, depression, anxiety, hopelessness . . . I already said stress, but will say it again: *stress*. Those options don't go away, and they don't have to.

My point: those contracted, lower-vibrational options that exist for our own humanness and for the rest of humanity don't have to go away in order for us to raise the ceiling on the Light that we are. Now, I'm not holding back here but treating you as the master that you are.

You may want to read the preceding portion again if the idea is new to you. In fact, you may need to reread it ten times before your brain will say, *Okay . . . wait, what?*

What I just said right there about the elevator was very important, because this awareness can prevent us from recreating an Atlantean implosion, which I know we're not here for. The violation of free will is a surefire way to implode all of the progress we've made.

We had to find a way to honor the free will of others while honoring our own free will of wanting to be a vessel of ever-increasing Light in our humanness, and we did. We did create a way, and that's what my Team and I call the Platinum Age.

Accessing the Full Range of the Keyboard

Now for step two in this upgraded view I'm wanting to convey, because—again—I'm not holding back.

Rather than looking at this frequency raising as being like an elevator, we're going to change the metaphor from an elevator car going up and down to a horizontal slide that goes from side to side, just like on our phones when we swipe the photos from right to left or left to right, or like any sort of volume knob that goes left to right when we're expanding, when we're adding more range.

We're making a bigger space between what's on the far left and what's on the far right. We're giving ourselves more room to be whatever we're choosing to be, but without removing any of the options.

Let's go with the idea of a piano. We have all the keys on the piano; I think there are eighty-eight. We've created a full keyboard, and we keep adding new keys.

Now, the old way of doing things, in the other Golden Ages, was that we said, "Let's make it easier for everybody. Let's take away those lower notes of the scale. We don't need those lower notes.

"They're sad . . . they're aggressive. They're not as happy. Let's only work with this end of the musical range. Let's take those other keys away so as not to distract anyone else, either, from the upper-range choices."

Can you feel the arrogance and elitism in that? I know that such judgment is not *my* cup of tea.

So here's the idea for those of us who are participating in the processes of this book. As we're expanding, let's keep remembering that we are the full range of the keyboard.

We could choose to be depressed in some moment, and it wouldn't be a terrible thing.

We still have all this expansion to work with, but we can still easily choose from that other range of notes if we want to for whatever reason, consciously or unconsciously. They're still there.

Because we're mature adults, we don't need to take the lower keys away so that we won't choose them. We can play there. Our Higher Selves aren't worried about us playing there at all. It's part of the full range of the human experience, and others are still choosing to live there.

We have the full range of the notes on the piano, and we're continuously adding more. We have an expanding keyboard of musical notes, of choices for how to be Light in our humanness. For this experience to be literally miraculous, we don't need to restrict ourselves or anyone else.

In summary, we don't need to raise the floor. I wanted to point that out to you because it *is* a novel concept. It's a very unique perspective, and, from what I'm being shown, it's important for everyone to know that. Not everyone does, so we'll just do our part.

Going back to everything we've done so far in this book, and about the sharing of this information, I do encourage you, or anyone else who wants to share this information with other people, to please feel free to do so.

If you're with me on social media, there are a whole lot of different ways that you can retweet or repost or share or like or comment on this information, from your perspective, to invite others in. Because, in that Chamber of Light, what they're showing me right now is that a lot of the seats aren't yet occupied.

No one was sitting there, and that's unfortunate. I'm speaking of the ones who actually had a spot all ready for them. *Or a spot will be made for them,* the Andromedan ambassador just offered. So your sharing about this book with others is deeply appreciated by the Team. I appreciate it, too.

The process of the Chamber of Light, the seaming—everything—is very important from what I can see, and I trust that many of you realize this, too. These messages are timeless, meant for far beyond the publication year of 2018.

Thank you for having you as your human here. Thank you for creating a seat for yourself, and for taking your seat. I'm so excited for where we'll go from here in this book.

For now, you might really let yourself reflect on the importance of this moment. Your experience was very real. And there's very little out in your outer world, whatever you're going off to do when you set down this book, that will match what you just did here.

It's up to each one of us to hold that energy for the rest of the planet. Remember that we're in this expanded energy range because the world doesn't know what we just did here, didn't choose to experience what we chose to create here, and probably wouldn't begin to grasp what we did here.

This world wasn't made to see us, especially in this way. My solution to that is, I don't ask it to. So it's our own job to see ourselves.

We're not asking this world to do anything but what it's doing, while we're asking ourselves to do what we do. We don't need anyone's validation that we're different, that we're upgraded. We're beyond that, right? That's the mature mastery that we're talking about here!

Yeah . . . you just be you.

Chapter Five
Restoring Humanity's Sovereignty

I love my work. One of the many reasons that I do is because I see your mastery—your Higher Self energy. And when we allow ourselves to see that mastery in ourselves, amazing things happen. We really start to have the breakthroughs that we've been wanting and waiting for, sometimes for our whole lives. So let's just get right into it.

Here we go. I invite you into the space of your Light within you, and let's go into those inner chambers of ourselves, of our Higher Self within ourself. Let's just relax everything, and when you finish reading about the following process, please close your eyes to go into the process.

Relax those shoulders and get nice and comfortable, to allow your human at all layers of you to be at ease, or at least at all the layers that you'll allow.

Let yourself absorb all of the pure Light, pure divinity, that you are in this world, just relaxing there and taking a lovely deep breath. Imagine that underneath your skin, within that flesh and bone, is just this radiating pure Light.

Very good. Take another nice, deep breath, relaxing those shoulders even more. Very good. Okay. Please put a smile on your face, if you haven't already.

I'd like you to imagine that, as you're looking more closely at the Light, kind of smiling at it, examining it, you realize that it's pure diamond energy. It also has some plasma qualities to it. It's alive, this Light. It's not still at all.

It's moving like a river. It's pumping like a heart, like blood from your heart. It's a vibrant energy. It seems happy, this Light in you. And what we wish to point out to you is that this Light was fully engaged at the moment you were even born. It's been running there, under the surface, all the while, even when you're doing other things.

Even when you're feeling like you're not doing your best, even when you feel like you could do more, even when you wish that you could do more, this Light of eternal energy is right there.

Its energy field, its source, goes far beyond this reality. It goes far beyond the reach of our brains, far beyond our ability to fully comprehend what it is, why it's there, how it got there, or what would work best for it.

It just is, and every time we're having a tough time it wants to give us the biggest hug. It wants to comfort us and lovingly tell us that it's going to be okay.

You're amazing, even if you don't feel it right now. This Light at your core is marvelous, and you don't need to earn it. It's yours. It was always yours. Your mastery is coded within this Light.

You can open your eyes again, if you haven't already.

Forget Everything You Thought You Knew

At this point, the Team and I would like to ask you something important, and it may seem weird but there's a method in this strange question.

We'd like to ask you to forget everything that you thought you knew about spirituality and about Light, or to at least push it a little bit to the side.

We're talking about all that learning, all that seeking, all that amazing knowledge, everything you've been told by other spiritual teachers or maybe even told yourself about this world and how it works and how to move it forward.

If you don't want to forget it for this experience, at least just push it to one side . . . as if you're at a dining room table and clearing some space for something new. Because we have many things to tell you that are very new.

The reason this is important is that, as we're switching over from the Third Dimension and launching this new Platinum Age, we have extra latitude for game changing, for altering courses. In other words, for changing the trajectory.

There's more wild-card energy in there, is how Archangel Metatron wants us to put it.

And the reason it's important to push to the side some of the things you thought you knew is that, in many cases regarding some of those things we thought we knew, we have already decided at a superconscious level that they haven't been bringing the results we wanted them to.

So when we say please put them to the side, please for a while imagine that they're not true. It's not someone outside of you saying, "Hey, you're wrong about that, you were always wrong about that." (Well, that can happen, and you can decide to agree or disagree.)

But, more importantly, many of you readers, as your superconscious self, amid your Higher Self energy, have been in Galactic Council meetings very similar to the one that took place in the Chamber of Light.

In those Galactic Council meetings, we discuss our human selves on another level of us, saying things like, "Hey this isn't working. We're trying to do this, we're trying to do that, I'm trying to feel better about this, trying to feel my Light in this way. We want our world to be like this and it isn't working."

And it's not like we're complaining. (Well, it does seem like some of us are complaining. But some of us have more just the attitude of, "I think we can do better than this.")

As the human representative of myself, and as one member of the human race, connected to this eternal Light, I might say, "I'm pretty sure we can do better than this, don't you agree?"

And then we discuss it, we strategize, and we come up with game plans. Many times, what we're doing is reevaluating.

"Okay, yes—so that pattern that I'm running for me and myself and what I'm contributing to humanity is attached to a truth of such and such, or attached to a belief that we are magnets and we're attracting energy, as compared to the upgraded truth that we are Creator beings. We're not magnets, we are Creator energy. We created magnets."

Beyond the Law of Attraction

We created something called the Law of Attraction, to see if it would be a truth that would serve us and move us forward. And you know what? In many ways it did move us forward from where we were before.

But now some of us are reflecting on it and saying, "Hey, wait a minute. It doesn't have that power any more. It actually feels, at this point of our consciousness, like a limitation. It feels like it doesn't help us access our sovereignty as much as we thought it would, or should, or could."

Or "You know what? I think we can do better. I think we're more than magnets. I think we do more than just attract. I think we might create!"

Do you see what I'm saying?

So (I'm saying this to your ego) it doesn't have to mean that we're saying, "You're wrong. You've always been wrong, you dummy," or anything like that. We're just wanting to expand the opportunity for you to experience yourself in this world.

There may be things that your beautiful ego (the ego being the storyteller) has attached itself to. It's keeping you at a rate of spin that is the revolutions per minute of your Light in your human energy field.

It's keeping you at a limit where you don't *want* to limit.

The Light of God in You

Okay, let's relax those shoulders again. Take another deep breath here, please. We're about to go back into Galactic Council chambers, and what we just discussed is very relevant to that.

45

Many of us are here because we want to be a part of these discussions. We want to feel it in our humanness, that we do play a role in the orchestrating of this world, that we matter.

We want to know that, in our lives, we guide energy and create energy every day. We want to verify that our thoughts and beliefs and sense of who and what we individually and collectively are goes hand-in-hand with how that Light core energy flows and grows and guides and shares and creates in this reality we call Earth.

It all goes together. And we're going to give you a tip. With every truth, with every belief that you know to be true, or that you wish were true and want to be true because you feel like it would be progressive and expansive, one of the best indicators of whether it truly is expansive and progressive is this. Does it honor that Light of God that we connected with in the very beginning of these processes?

Does it recognize that it's there? Does it honor the fact that it's yours and always was yours, and you don't need to earn it back or learn it back? It's an always-on infrastructure of your eternal source energy, and it is trustworthy.

Beautiful. Now this Light in you is like a beautiful pillar, standing tall and proud within your energy field, not in an arrogant way but in an owning-it kind of way. You might even want to imagine that your human is standing again in the foyer of that Chamber of Light where we were before, and looks like a beautiful column.

See the columns of time that have held up great buildings in this world, and the column of Light built and created just for you by your Higher Self, for this lifetime, for your human journey right now. There are no holes in it, no gaps. It's rock solid.

We can feel the energy in the foyer starting to rise, as we know that it's nearly the time of commencement. And again those doors, those beautiful, crystalline doors with emerald handles, are magically opening by themselves and we are floating into the chamber again, knowing we have a seat and feeling guided directly to it by our Light. Our Light knows directly where to go.

So again you're in your seat. It feels like home, feels like the seat was made for you—because it was. Make yourself comfortable there. Get yourself acquainted energetically with this space prepared just for you in this chamber. Again we can feel all the energies of our galactic people and other contingencies who look and feel familiar, giving rise to a feeling of "Oh, yeah . . . *you* guys!"

And we may be laughing at the fact that we don't yet even remember about "those guys" in our human awareness. They haven't even come up yet, and the others are laughing at that, but the forgetting of humanity, the veiling, is such a wondrous, ingenious process, and they're honoring it.

They're not saying, "Oh my gosh, you don't even remember about us?"

It's more like, "Yeah, what a ride, right? You guys are awesome for being there, and being *here* you're rock stars!"

It's all well and good, all divinely designed to be exactly as it is. Do some deep breathing here, please.

The Voice of the Collective Team

One voice now speaks for the assembled Team.

We call to order this special assembly in the Chamber of Light, again welcoming the humans, so delighted that you are hands-on in this process. We welcome all of your humanness, knowing what a neat package it is for your beautiful, eternal Light. A Source Creator God is what you always have been, always will be, and are even presently, in your humanness.

We care what you think. You're beautiful ambassadors of the human race in this experience. Just as our partner Jill was offering earlier about your experiences in the Galactic Council meetings, where you show up to join the discussion, all of you have been there multiple times in those council meetings. And it's okay that your human doesn't remember. It wasn't made to remember things like that.

It's not necessary for you, as your human, to remember any Galactic Council meeting that you've been a part of on any level of you.

It's important that we offer that, to help you acknowledge, to help you expand into the knowing, that you haven't been helpless, that humanity is not helpless, that the biggest struggle humanity faces, and that you may also be struggling with in some ways, is the fighting against the veils. It's the conclusion that the veils are awful, terrible, have been done to you, and that they must be removed.

That's a story that will keep you, and has actually kept humanity, within that parking-garage structure that you've been in. That thinking has been keeping humanity at that same vibrational range for not just decades, not just hundreds of years, not just thousands of years, but way further back. (A big sigh from our partner Jill, here, on that one.)

Please speak out loud to yourself, or in an inner voice— however you choose—the feelings that brings up for you. Give voice to the emotions of anger, frustration, confusion, that some of you may be feeling about that. Some of your beautiful, intelligent minds are saying, "But but but but," wanting to argue with that truth. And so there are two beings coming forward to the podium, right alongside me as the present spokesperson, who want to shed some Light on this subject.

Jesus is here first. And he has that special, human Jesus smile that is only his.

Chapter Six
Jesus and Mary Magdalene

I see you and I welcome you, and I celebrate the fact that you're here, including your own humanness here in this experience by way of Jill's book. You should be extremely pleased with yourself for your ability to bypass the veils in order to get yourself here . . . that's interstellar, right there!

I want to offer compassion, understanding, healing, and grace to any part of you that doesn't want that to be true. That doesn't want to believe and doesn't want to know and wants it to be wrong that, forever, since Earth was created, there has been a truth—or there has been a mistruth, there's been a belief, an application of logic—that the veils had to be removed.

And some of you are saying, "But what about Atlantis, what about this, what about that, what about Lemuria? What about all those amazing timelines?"

Do you know what happened in those timelines that some of you so badly want back or want to create another even better version of? They didn't fight the veils.

You got here today, participating in this Chamber of Light as your human, because you realized at some level that there were parts of you that didn't remember, parts of you that maybe didn't need to remember.

You wondered: What if all you had to do was know that you are eternally Light, claim that Light and the power of it, and just work with that, start there? What if that was enough?

And it was, because it got you here! And it got us there. In my journey, that's what I did.

Now, I know that history changed my life dramatically. Human history, especially with that veiling we've been talking about, has a funny way of doing that.

Buddha just said, "Amen!" He'll be up soon, by the way, and Mary Magdalene wants to speak as well, and of course we're excited for both speakers.

So you are here despite the fact that there is veiling within you. Humanity and life on Earth were created with the system of veiling in order for there to be a human experience, in order for humanity to be able to forget that it was God.

The story about me is that there were no parts of me that were veiled—that I was completely one with Source Creator God. I may disappoint some of you when I say that this wasn't true, and it still isn't true. It wasn't true then and it isn't true now.

*Mother Mary is smiling, saying, "I can attest to that,"
and Mary Magdalene is laughing as she says, "So can I!"*

*There were parts of me, as Jesus, that remained uncon-
scious, and I didn't let it bother me. Now, some of you
may call that shadows, some may name that inner-child
work. Some of you may think of it as soul-retrieval opportunities. There are a whole bunch of very sophisticated
and relevant terms to apply to what happens when a part
of you is veiled.*

*At some point in my journey, I realized that I was pure
Light, and yet I still had parts of me that were veiled. I
could get angry. I could get frustrated. I could get stubborn. I could get distracted.*

*I wanted to be alone a lot, and that was confusing to
those who wanted to hear more of what I had to say . . .
those who wanted to know how I was able to be my pure
Light.*

*There were times when I felt owned by those who
wanted more from me, and I didn't like that feeling. It
felt draining. It felt like I was being fed off of, and I didn't
like it.*

*So I needed to kind of create my own space, so that I
could also appreciate the human journey I was having.
Not in a selfish way, but in the sense of, "Hey, I don't feel
like I can be that. I don't feel like I can be my own Light
in the way that I have figured out how to be, if I'm being
fed off of energetically so often."*

*Many of you can relate to this, yes? When I look at
each of you, I see that every one of you, in not just one*

way but multiple ways, has known, perhaps even more strongly as a child, that you had something special inside of you.

And you're right. That is still true. That Light within you that we connected with at the very beginning of this experience today is unlike any other.

Jesus: I Allowed My Light to Prevail

If you could see each other's Light, you would chuckle or giggle and say, "Oh, my Gosh, look at yours . . . oh, here, look at mine," and you'd smile and be so in awe of your own and each other's Light. They are different; they're not the same!

It's as if you were to spend time staring into each other's eyes and then have a mirror and stare into your own. Everyone's eyes are amazing. None of them are the same. With fingerprints it's the same thing: everyone's fingerprints are unique. Nobody's DNA is the same; even the spiral of the DNA is different.

There are so many unique traits to each and every one of you. We love to point out how amazing that is, that there are so many facets of you that are verifiably—and even in a court of law, for evidence—unique, one-of-a-kind facets of who you are as your human. And that ties directly to your Higher Self energy. Your Higher Self is every bit as unique and one-of-a-kind.

So, at the most expanded realms of divine energy, there's no need for names or name tags because the recognition and acknowledgment of uniqueness is so obvious and so prevalent. In our divine systems of communication and interaction, there's no need for us to go by a name.

This is why it's fun for me to be called Jesus. It's like returning to your hometown, where when you were young everybody called you something else. When you get there, it's like, "Oh, yeah—that's right! I remember that. I remember being called Jimmy instead of James, or Little Jimmy or Junior or something like that, [laughing], and then you're in that feeling again.

I have such good memories . . . even with what happened. I have such fond memories of being Jesus. That was a great life.

There are probably things I'd do differently. There were moments when I wish more people would have heard me. It was hard to see people suffer. Unconsciousness can be a really ugly thing; I know that each of you can relate to that pretty easily. That's hard.

That, to me, was the most difficult part of being human, especially with the type of consciousness that I had—and the level of consciousness that you also have, that has you here, engaging consciously with us in a Chamber of Light.

Witnessing from your humanness, which can also feel like helplessness, another person's or even your own pain and suffering, amid the veils, especially, is extremely hard and can be very painful. That's why we're here.

That's why these Galactic Council meetings are here: not necessarily for therapy, but for solution making. "What can we do? What if we tried this? Would it reduce the suffering if we did that? Would it reduce the pain for our own Light body, that's wearing this human experience on the outside?

"Is there something else we can do so that we don't feel the pain so much? Let's play with that, let's experiment. Let's get in the 'lab' and play with our Light and our energy field, play with our mental body, play with our emotional body. Let's experiment, let's explore. Let's see if there's another way to do this."

I had human pain as Jesus, obviously, and still I allowed my Light to prevail. I allowed my Light to be real, and to prevail, no matter what.

Maybe that would work for you. I see each of you as a master, so I'm not going to use this opportunity to dictate to you how to do it.

But I also love you enough, definitely, to share with you what worked really well for me. When I allowed my Light to prevail, to be strong, to be sturdy, to be real, to be relevant, no matter what else was going on in my human life or in the reality at large, everything changed for me.

Everything changed for me, and maybe it will for you. Maybe it will get even better for you.

Okay—we're having a background discussion here, because there's a point that we want to get to, relative to a situation that's prevailed since the beginning of time on Earth. It's about this kind of locked-in set of energy and how that doesn't have to be a problem, so we're debating about who gets to talk about that . . . whether it's me, Buddha, Mary Magdalene . . .

Mary says she wants to, so we're going to switch gears here. Thank you for being here. Thank you for being you. Thank you for letting me share with you from this part of myself. Thank you for letting me play Jesus again—that's fun. I love that guy!

Mary Magdalene: An Insatiable Desire for Light

Hello! Here I am at the podium with a big smile on my face. Talk about veiling, and about service being hijacked! I still tease my partner Jill that, for the first thirty-eight years—longer than that—for the first many years of her life, she knew me as the prostitute in the New Testament.

We still have a good laugh about that, and about how that veil worked. She doesn't judge herself for having taken literally the New Testament of the Bible. She just loves it that it was wrong. [Laughs.] There is so much more to me, and there was even when I was Mary, than that part of the story.

That's okay. It's not bothering me, and not bothering Jill, that probably most of the planet still thinks of me that way. Those who are stuck (in self-imposed stuckness, but they don't know it) within that locked-in energy range that keeps them in that parking-garage structure and not extending beyond it, are allowing old energy patterns to keep them there.

Now, with a group like this, what's important to also know is that, since the beginning of time, there have been individuals who have created ways of unlocking themselves from that system. They questioned, they explored, they were curious, they were stubborn [laughing again], *and they kept going. They were unsatisfied, perhaps with their present-day teachings.*

They were angry that the teachings didn't have the positive effect they thought they should have, especially when it comes to something like spirituality or enlightenment, progressivism . . . it's been named so many things, and has even gone beyond names, from the beginning of time.

A series of humans have literally incarnated with an insatiable desire for Light, and yet have somehow held the accompanying recognition that there are veils.

They somehow realized that the Light and the veils were going to go together; they didn't know how yet, but somehow they were going to go together.

There is actually, at the Higher Self levels, some degree of excitement about that. And this group gathered here, all of our Higher Selves, is very similar. We are mavericks. We're rebellious in some ways.

I mean, just consider the idea that an entire group like this, including myself, Jesus, Buddha—everyone in this entire chamber who has ever incarnated into humanity— has worn this little smile, as if to say, "Yeah, but I brought some secrets."

Mary Magdalene: Light and Veils Coexisting

Yes, I was going to be veiled, but I was also coding myself in multiple ways, with backup plans upon backup plans upon backup plans, not to remove all the veils, because Earth wasn't created for that.

But I would have enough ways of questioning and creating and exploring, as well as this passion for Light and well-being for myself and others, that it would keep guiding me beyond the boundaries of what humanity presently was during my incarnation.

Each time I took birth, I was going to push the envelope from the moment I was born.

I might do it on the sly, where only my mother knew that I had this other side to me (which some of you can probably relate to).

Or there could be another version of it where everyone knew, like, "Oh, that little troublemaker," when we were small.

Jesus has this funny thing to share, and I think you're going to love it, too. He's saying, "I was the troublemaker from the moment I was born, and my mother knew it.

"Yet isn't it ironic that my followers (those who follow the teachings of Christ, which have been very manipulated for the separation age) seem to consider themselves the ones who follow the rules.

They are good little church girls and boys. They go to church on Sunday. They follow the rules to the letter of the law, when none of that is what I did. Are you laughing, too, at the irony of that?"

He can't stop laughing, and I'm laughing as he is. He's not making fun of the Christians as a group; it's just that the irony is so rich.

With some of us, everybody would say, "Oh, that one. That one is never going to follow the rules. I worry about that one." And, of course, what we were probably thinking was, "You're worried about me? You should be worried about yourself, because you're only following the rules here on Earth."

However it was that you wired yourself uniquely, it's important to acknowledge that uniqueness of your Light, while also honoring and celebrating the uniqueness of you as your Higher Self.

That uniqueness makes Source infinite, for each of us is a subcreation within the overall Source Creator God energy field. We want to push that envelope, too—that's what makes Source infinite versus contained and static and not growing.

Mary Magdalene: A Family of Troublemakers

We're doing this on multiple levels. We do it in our human incarnation and we're doing it at our Higher Self level. We're a family of troublemakers in a lot of ways, and we really wouldn't want it any other way. That's an inappropriate term in some ways, because we really don't want to create trouble, but we are the ones who rock the boat, at all levels of ourselves.

And yet here we are in the Chamber of Light, in a very celebrated, highly regarded position of being. It's a position of authority, and one of Creator energy. It's a gathering of those of us who do things our own way.

We're offered, and we actually created, this Chamber of Light, and no one argued with us and no one could have held us back even if they tried. There's an understanding among the All That Is, that there are flavors of us that exist in order to keep Source Energy creative and expansive and infinite.

Please just feel that for a moment. There is a stillness in our partner Jill that she's never felt before, the acknowledgment that, even as her Higher Self, she wants more all the time. She wants more for herself. She wants more for everybody. It is a selfless desire.

We're not concerned, then, about how, since the beginning of the concept of Earth and humanity, there has been this idea of a locked game—what Jill has begun referring to as the quarantine. She's not concerned about that, not really. She might have been at some point. She might at some point have decided that it was our job to remove the quarantine.

No, it's your job, if you want to look at it that way, to hijack the quarantine, so that you can be the way you were coded to be. That way isn't fully unveiled, but it includes the recognition and declaration that you're fully Light, even amid the veils. And that, that's game changing.

So, yes, you are hijacking the quarantine, reprogramming Earth, and upgrading the human grid structure. You're upgrading Earth.

Gaia just said, "Amen!"

Yet you're doing it in such a way that you're allowing Earth to be exactly what she is. You're also allowing humanity to be exactly what it is, and that bothers some of you. Some of you really want more evidence that you're making a powerful difference in your fellow humans' lives right now, and that is of course your choice.

I just love you enough to also point out that it's not necessary for you to do it that way. I wouldn't be as satisfied with my life as Mary Magdalene had I felt that it was my job or my mission or even my opportunity to make others' lives better. I chose to look at my life as mine and other people's lives as their own.

Mary Magdalene: A Badge of Creation

I'll tell you what's perhaps the most difficult thing to imagine, even for the larger group here in the chamber. All of us here in this Chamber of Light find it challenging to appreciate and understand why another human, even as their Higher Self, wouldn't want to break out of that parking structure.

It's hard for us to imagine why others would feel satisfied there . . . why, even as their Higher Self in the All That Is, there is this strange contentment with what is. Why there isn't this curiosity that asks, "But what if we tried it another way?"

It's as if they look back at us to say, "But why would you want to try it another way? What's wrong with the way things are right now? Why do you keep trying to rewrite things? Why do you consistently want to recreate things, to do it another way by taking it apart and putting it back together again in a different way?

"Why do you do that?" they ask. "Why do you consume so much energy? Why do you want to take pleasure in contemplating and envisioning and creating new things that haven't been there before?"

Within the All That Is, there is far more energy related to stabilizing the Light and appreciating the Light that's been created, compared to a proportionally smaller group of energy that absolutely delights in the fact that Source is infinite, and that this infinity gives Source a hall pass of authority, a badge of creation to use in many, many ways.

Mary Magdalene: There's Nothing to Fix Here

So the misunderstanding that many of you hold, relative to your fellow humans, about what you see as their pain, their suffering, or their struggle, is that you want to fix it. And that's what some of us, in a different way, feel at the Higher Self level. Because we wonder, "Really? You're just happy with the way it is? What's wrong with you?"

Now, in the humanness again, related to what Jesus was mentioning, it's different. Because, at the Higher Self level, there's not the pain-and-suffering component because there's not the veiling.

You who are living Earth lives have the veiling and the quarantine effect, and also a level of constraint within that parking-garage range of energy that is so tight and so narrow that there is much pain and suffering, because it's painful to be separate from your Source energy.

And, in the ways that humanity has created or has been using since the beginning, different attempts have been made, while staying within the confines, the limitations, of that parking structure, to try to make sense of it.

That's why many of you were discontent with the organized religions of this world, by the way. You knew at a soul level that that wasn't the whole story, that something about it was not quite right.

You sensed that it was not honoring of the Light of God within you, and that it wasn't honoring of the Light within others, either. But, for some people, it does provide a service to unconsciousness. There is this attitude of, "Well, it's working for me." They, for some reason, haven't contemplated that there's something else there, that something else is available. It's amazing.

For those of you who, in your humanness, feel an urge to do something about that unconsciousness, go for it. It can provide you with a lot of experimentation. It keeps Source infinite, trying to pull those folks out of that limited parking-garage structure.

Some may hear you. Some may hear you temporarily (either feeling their own Light or feeling yours) and seemingly pop out of that parking structure to allow more of their Light, and then they may go back into the safety of the confines of that parking garage.

They may kind of pop out but then go back in, and then, like a turtle, pop out and then go back in to the safety of the shell. They are just not wired the way that you are, and perhaps the hardest truth for some of you to hear is that they don't have to be. At their Higher Self level, many of them are very similar. There's nothing to fix here, in that regard.

At their Higher Self level, they are still choosing to incarnate here. That's why they're here; there is still obviously some sense of purpose and relevance in that experience. It is a trip to forget that you're God, so Earth serves that purpose going forward.

But then, what is the Platinum Age? If it's been this way since the beginning of time, then what is different right now? Why wouldn't this shift that many of you have accurately sensed be any different from any other Golden Age?

And now Lord Buddha is saying, "It's my turn."

Chapter Seven
Buddha: The Light Within You

So here we are, in this "Being Your Light" endeavor, with human representatives fully engaged in the Chamber of Light. To me, that alone makes this the Platinum Age, because this has never been done before. For that reason alone, I can't stop smiling.

And Jesus just teased me, saying, "Well, you can't stop smiling ever—that's true!"

What's wrong with smiling? To me, nothing!

I'm just taking my time here, appreciating the unique assembly of Light that I see, each of you so fully engaged in your humanness.

I'm noticing, with each and every one of you readers, the curious energy patterns of Earth that have you outside of yourself in some ways.

You are not usually reveling in that Light of God that is the pool of eternal energy within you, and yet I feel no judgment about that discord.

I feel nothing but honor for the fact that you are an eternal wellspring of Light as your Higher Selves and as your humanness, and that your humanness gets to somehow put it all together in a way that works for you.

I hope that what we've shared so far has given you more permission to loosen up any attachment to some of those truths and beliefs that have you holding yourself away from that Light within you, that have you holding your Light almost at arm's length.

We Know That It Can Be Lonely

But your Light is not outside of you; it's inside of you. So what it looks like energetically, by the way, is that it is as if you're off-center. When your human consciousness is off to the left or off to the right or up too high or down too low, relative to the core of Light that is literally at your center, that naturally happens on Earth.

It naturally happens at the veiling, and then that disconnection is kept in place by the truths and beliefs that allow the separation to even be. The veils are supported energetically by the truths and beliefs that humans tell themselves.

The beauty and the power is that those truths and beliefs can be erased, can be rewritten at any moment. But most of you aren't told that, because the human experience is set up for separation.

Our partner Jill wired herself to be like many of you, to hear the clarion call for how to be Light in this reality and bypass the nonsense, the shenanigans. She uses those derogatory terms just to keep herself entertained, because she is naturally rebellious. But, more than anything, she loves Light.

Jill doesn't like to see the pain and suffering in this world, especially among those who are so clearly declaring that they don't want to play the game the way it's been written.

She's looking for her fellow rule breakers. She's doing many things to shout out to the world, "Hey, if you don't like these rules either, let's play together. I've got some things figured out. You'll figure out some new things, together we'll figure out more new things, and together we'll rewrite this whole show—this whole way of being Light in this reality."

The fact that you're all here together in this Chamber of Light is another sign of success for all of you who like to break the rules. In other moments of linear time on Earth, it was just Jesus in this room, or just Jesus, Mary, and Mary Magdalene, or just a handful of the tribe of Light who were on Earth at that time.

In my time, it was just me, just the Buddha [laughing] *. . . I was the only human who was showing up. Humans have never shown up in this quantity before, although there were always seats for you here, waiting in readiness for you.*

We always hoped you'd be here, so please forgive me if I'm crying. Actually some of you may be able to notice and sense that there are many of us in this Chamber of Light in our own version of tears . . . tears of joy, tears of celebration, tears of compassion for what it took for you to break out of that system that's so well entrenched on Earth and that can be so hard.

We know that it can be lonely, that it can be isolating, that it can feel like you are one in a billion and even that number is an understatement. Jesus just said, "That is so true."

How We See You

We see you as an evolution of Light in human form. We see you as a genius for incarnating when you did. Not because Earth itself has changed (no offense meant to Gaia), but because the timing of the grand cycles of energy and the minor cycles of energy is in such a state right now that it actually allows more rule breaking. It allows for major transformation and forward leaps of human evolution.

Each of you created within yourself, when you were planning your journey—this human incarnation that you're having right now—multiple backup systems for how you would tend to reject the present-day ways of doing things. And that got you here. We hope you feel that as an accomplishment.

But, more importantly, where will you allow it to take you from here?

That is that special Light quality about you that is similar among each of you, as Mary just said to us. Even as your Higher Selves, every single one of you shares an attitude of, "Yes, but what else can we do? How can we make it better? What else can we try?"

It's to varying degrees, for certain, and yet there is that similar ingredient, and that is what got you here. That's to be celebrated, but we're not stopping there, and we know you aren't, either.

Because we know you have your own list of dreams and hopes and wishes—for yourself, in ways that you expect or even command that things will get better, and you may also have another version of the wish list for your fellow humans.

That one, again, I encourage you to be cautious with, because of the need in the human race to honor others' lives exactly as they are, honoring their Higher Self construct in the awareness that they're not you, so why ask them to be like you?

You can create some way of being you and being your Light, all bright and shiny, despite the pain and suffering that is a part of Earth.

But it's not all of Earth. That's not all of what's going on there. There's a lot of joy, a lot of hope. On Earth there is a lot of reveling in Light-based energies as well as the challenges, and it all goes together.

The fact that it all goes together is just miraculous; it literally is. That's what keeps a lot of us going back to Earth more than once, this amazingness of it. It's amazing and it is very true.

Every single one of you who expands beyond the boundaries of human grid laying, human Light-based energy ranges, every single one of you is hijacking that continuously because you want more, more, more. You want to figure out more ways to make the veils be less of an obstacle, to work around the veils, to thin the veils.

Meanwhile, you're still understanding that this is a quarantine, that there is unconsciousness even within yourself. And yet you're not letting that stop you. You know that you are also pure Light—eternal, soulful, and omnipresent.

Laying Tracks for Others to Follow

You knew that this could be amazing, and it is amazing! Every single one of you is wired that way. You are naturally wired to lay tracks, so that anyone else who cares to can follow in your footsteps.

I know that some of you reading this book have felt as if you were laying tracks for decades, and many times it might have felt very hard. There are also some in this Chamber of Light group who feel like they woke up not too long ago, like they awakened to that eternal pure Light of God within them more recently than others of you—the ones who have been doing this for decades.

I'm pointing out the contrast between the more recently awakened ones and those of you who have long felt as if you were always struggling uphill in trying to resurrect and restore that Light of God within yourselves, in a world that wasn't set up for that.

You laid tracks as you did that, and what that allowed to happen is that some of your fellow humans had a much easier time in their process of making their own self-discovery and creating their own awakening.

They didn't have to hit rock bottom. They didn't have to have a painful dark night of the soul. In fact, Jill doesn't even personally know, as Jill, what a dark night of the soul is.

That doesn't mean she's not as expanded as she is. It means she's been able to skip some of the steps. Do you know why? Because some of you laid tracks that allowed her to bypass that pain-and-suffering part of awakening. How cool is that? And she's saying thank you to all of you readers who did that.

So, even in this Chamber of Light, you have greatly assisted each other, even in your own lifetimes And I also want to say, on behalf of anyone who might have benefited directly from your process, thank you.

Thank you for leaving a doorway where there wasn't one before—that place where you broke through and left a big ol' hole there for anyone else to plow through when they wanted to. Thank you for doing that. Thank you for being you. It allowed you to be in this chamber, and not by yourself. Thank you.

Heavy Lifting

There is a standing ovation for you, by the way. And this is important.

For those of you who know that, so far in your incarnation, you've been doing a lot of heavy lifting in this reality, and who for a long, long time were talking about things that no one even knew existed, you deserve this recognition.

Thank you for your service of Light to the planet when you might not even have known what you were doing, when you perhaps just sensed that something was seriously wrong and you wanted to create something that was right. From our perspective, you succeeded beautifully. These accolades are well earned.

So now, for those of you who have perhaps skated through a little more easily than others, what we notice about you (and we're talking to our partner in this as well), is this. Just because you skated through what had been obstacles to some of your comrades here, notice that you're putting to good use that expanded, less damaged, less fragmented Light, because you're a different version of pure energy who isn't as disenfranchised, doesn't have as much of a chip on your shoulder.

We're not taking anything away from those who did the heavy lifting, but do you notice the difference? You show up here differently, yes?

Some of you want to talk about war stories, while some of you don't have as many war stories to tell. But what I'm getting at is the fact that those who feel, or may look, like they skated through . . . trust me. You're creating your own war stories, because you're using that Light to penetrate to the next boundary level that you sense.

Right now you're seeing dimensions of boundaries that others may not see. And you're seeing those on behalf of everyone else, just like the ones with the war stories did. Does that make sense?

So no one is getting bypassed. No one's getting left in the dust. Everybody is being pulled outward, which really means pulled inward, closer to that Light of God energy. And you're all working together, even when you don't know that you are.

Some of you, decades ago, felt as if you were literally in a mine, kind of chipping away and wondering, "Am I making a difference?" I know that Jill feels that way a lot when she sees so-called truths that 98 percent of spiritual people are walking around with, such as the Law of Attraction or The Secret.

And she's looking at those beliefs and thinking, "But that's not right. There's something seriously wrong about The Secret. *There's something seriously wrong about the Law of Attraction. Within herself she's saying, "There's something wrong about this. Wait! No, it's really* this!

And she asks herself, "How do I tell them this? How do I share with this amazing, sophisticated group of humans that there is even more? How do I do this without coming across as judgmental? How do I do it without dishonoring the fact that they figured out something that worked? How do I do this when I know that there is more and I don't know how to tell them that there is more?"

We can tease our partner, because she's not too sensitive about it and she's kind of laughing at it, too.

Jill is saying, "It's true. It's true that we all have our own version of chipping away at the armor of humanity and parting the veils of the quarantine for the purpose of making more room for this eternal Light of God."

It's such a strange and fascinating and wonderful reality, all at the same time. It really is.

You Needn't Have the Same Passions

There are many facets of this human experience that each of you individually, and perhaps many of you collectively, want to change in this reality. But you don't always agree on what those changes should be.

There can be discomfort in that, because it's easier to imagine that you're all on the same page and you all see things the same way. But the unique mastery that's here among this group of readers is very obvious to us, and in time your own mastery may become more obvious to each of you.

You don't all have to care about the same things. You needn't have the same passions about what could be better on Earth, or what could be better even for yourself or others. Each of you, as the mavericks that you are, did create, in many ways, these sort of special projects— powerful experiments that you wanted to play with.

So many of you are experimenting and exploring. We hear you say, "I wonder, if I'm this way, if I can make a difference with this.

And you say, "I wonder, if I'm that way, if I can make a difference with that."

Where it becomes separative, where it becomes a barrier to your expanding beyond that parking-garage structure, is when your passions keep you from accepting the eternal Light of God that you are right now in your humanness.

You could look at it as A: There's a flaw, or B: There's a problem, or C: It's fine just where it is, depending on your objective. We see the potential in each of you, and your natural wiring to consistently be wanting to add more Light into this reality.

Chapter Eight
Buddha: Free Will Is Free Will

For those of us on the Team, it does feel like a mismatch when any sort of belief has you in an energy pattern of, "Oh, my gosh, we'll be able to accept so much more Light of God when this is fixed . . . when that group is well . . . when that other group is protected . . . when every group is safe and secure."

That's not true; those views are not accurate. There has been pain and suffering on planet Earth since the very beginning. And that actually surprised us.

I'm just speaking from the Creation Team energy here, which many of you were a part of, by the way. We didn't know what was going to happen on Earth—we really didn't. So, when the incarnations started to happen, human or otherwise, and the veiling happened, then of course we were observing it.

But, because of the way that we set up the quarantine and the way that free will operates within the quarantine, there's only so much that we can do. So we felt helpless in some ways, too, because we looked at our representatives, human or otherwise, and felt like, "Oh no, wow. They really forgot everything."

"Darn it, those veils are good," is what we said to each other. "Well, now what do we do?" Thus we were experimenting, exploring, and monitoring, but realizing that free will is free will and that we set it up that way.

So we admit that there were times when we actually wanted that physical journey, whatever it was, to be over. Like, "Oh, please, let it just be done so that they can have their life review. I can rush it to them and say, 'Let me let you back in again. Okay, here we go, you're good, it's all good. It was just a dream. That's not who you really are. You aren't really in pain, you aren't really suffering, it's all good.'"

There's this hyperventilating sort of experience of the physical you, at that moment, of the adrenaline pumping. And the etheric body adrenaline rushes through. Adrenaline is amazing, an amazing force of energy that works with the human body and even with that of the expanded energy field. Yet it doesn't always lead to joy, and that's where the free will thing came in.

We were asking ourselves, "Wow, why did they choose pain and suffering? Oh, that's right. They didn't know they were choosing it. My gosh, this reality is really crazy and good and scary all at the same time."

You Are Counseled before You Incarnate

So, especially at the beginning, there were times when we wished we could pluck that human or that physical form out of there to save them. But we realized that, by using cycles of incarnation, they were going on and on and on, and that they were fine.

Any energy seemingly lost was restored (reunioned— that's not a word, but we just made it up) after the "death" of that physical journey. We realized that all were fully restorable, and that the experiences did add to the collective.

If we, as our Higher Selves, had on Earth a human representative or any sort of animal or plant life, when that restoration happened, when that physical journey was over, there was infinite expansion. Any pain and suffering ended, once that energy field had fully detached from the quarantine experience.

So we learned in that process that, for some, it can really be awful—whether at moments or for almost the whole journey while they're there. Yet we now give even more forewarning. I mean, before you incarnate, trust me: there is a lot of counseling, and you enter into a lot of "disclosure agreements."

For example: "Now, you know that anything could happen here. You've done your homework, yes? You know that the pain and suffering on Earth can be unlike anything you can imagine. You've researched how it's gone for other people."

Still, there is this eager sort of excitement in the eyes of the Higher Self energy, as if to say, "I know, I know. But

I also know that I'm fine, because I've done that before. I've had some crazy lives on Earth."

Again, we're not just talking about humans. For every single Higher Self energy that decides to incarnate an aspect of itself, their Higher Self is whole and complete the whole time. While that physical journey, on Earth or anywhere else, is taking place, they're not feeling, "Oh, I'm not complete because I've got a human down there" or "I've got an animal life version of me down there."

They are whole and complete. They're fine, and they're noticing when that physical self has a good time or a bad time or a tough moment or an amazing moment. It's all reflective. They can see it; they can sense it.

We know it's going on. And yet there's only so much that we can do, especially while that journey is in motion. Then, after the life review, we're the first one there to say, "Okay, I'm you and you're actually me, do you remember now?" And sometimes that adjustment takes a while.

Earth Is Much More Than a Dream

So there is forewarning, and Earth is a very, very unique place. From our Higher Self perspective, it is more like a dream state.

If you see someone you love who's having a bad dream, do you wake them up? It's okay either way. But do you wake them up, or do you simply remember that it's a dream?

It's real, but at the same time it's not real. It's just real enough to let the dreamer have an actual experience, yet when the dream is over there's fogginess about what really happened.

Earth is much more than a dream. It's not a hologram in the way that some humans say, to infer that it doesn't matter. Earth is very real, and the experiences it offers are very, very real. The spectrum of experiences available on Earth is unlike what we would have predicted, yet we've decided over and over again to not shut it down.

There are still willing participants in the experience, as incomprehensible as that might seem from within your human experience right now. We get it, that it's inconceivable when someone you know is suffering, or when you are undergoing your own personal suffering.

At some point you say, "I can't have known that it was going to be this bad. I've got to be smarter than that as my Higher Self. I mean, what idiot of a Higher Self would incarnate here knowing that this suffering was a possibility? What the heck is wrong with me?"

But that way of thinking doesn't match how your Higher Self is thinking about it at all, at all. Even in the pain, even in the suffering, there is so much other energy going on in your humanness right alongside it. It all can go together.

The Experience of Jesus on the Cross

Jesus was literally hanging on a cross with nails in his wrists and nails in his ankles and feet. Was he in pain? Hell, yes. Did it feel like hell on Earth? Yes. Was he at the same time praying for humanity and forgiving those who had done that to him? Yes.

Was he feeling a sense of euphoria alongside the pain, as strange as that may sound? Yes, he was. The experience was forcing him, in many ways, to tap into an even deeper human connection with that Light that we got to at the beginning here.

Jesus knew that he needed that Light really badly, because being killed and being aware of it is not a pleasant process for any human life in which that happens. A slow death is never fun, true?

The connection of feeling and senses and emotions with it has a whole range of experience. It doesn't have to be in that parking-garage structure, but it can be and it actually most often is, as you can imagine. But it doesn't have to be.

So there is even an upgraded way of perceiving pain and suffering—your own or that of others—where one can find the sense of honor for the Higher Self energy that is in there, even when they don't know it's in there. That eternal Light of God is present and always on, even when an individual doesn't know it's on, even when they've never heard that it was on and may never imagine that it's on, may never connect to it in their entire physical journey.

You're seeing it; you're seeing their Light of God, not their pain and suffering. You're knowing that their eternal energy field is in there, even amid that pain, that suffering, and it can serve a great purpose. Some of you are up for that challenge, and some of you are saying, "I can't do that. I can't be me and do these other things that

I'm really passionate about if I'm staring at the face of pain and suffering every day."

Some of you are wired that way. For some of you it's a passion; for others it isn't. Don't ask yourselves to agree among yourselves that that's relevant. You are all wired so differently in this life.

We Honor You

All right, it was important that we got to that, and I'm glad that we did.

We're feeling led to start to wrap things up here in this Being Your Light endeavor. So let's put a bit of a seal on the Chamber of Light experience.

Oh—the other group never got their applause; thank you! The Pleiadians just said, "We gave the applause for the ones that have been laying tracks seemingly for decades, but we didn't give the standing ovation to those who look like they skated in, and we want to. Despite appearances, they're doing their own heavy lifting."

Everyone's doing heavy lifting; that's why you got here to this Chamber, yes?

But that is a challenge for all of you, so for those who feel as if they didn't have as hard a road, it's your turn. Thank you, thank you, for pushing the envelope.

Thank you for realizing that there was an envelope to push, where others sometimes didn't even see that there was a problem. That's a curious place to be. We honor you and appreciate you. Your unique way of assisting Light in this reality is deeply appreciated and deeply honored.

From our perspective, we covered a lot today, and the energetic attunements that take place all the while you're reading were very deep. When we look at you and at the Light at your core, that Light now feels brighter and more vibrant.

It feels even more alive than it did before, and, from our perspective, readers, your human energy field feels more bright and curious and creative, and more empowered to play with that eternal Light even more powerfully, even more purposefully, with even more self-respect and self-recognition and perhaps even more joy. We hope so.

We honor you, and this Chamber of Light session of the Galactic Council, of the Platinum rays and Golden rays and many other rays too numerous to mention, has concluded. Light activations complete, and so it is.

Chapter Nine
Our Life-giving Soulfulness

I've loved what has come through for us from Jesus, Mary Magdalene, and Buddha. I hope that you have, too. There was a lot there!

I'll also share, as human Jill, that a lot of it was new for me. I had never thought about this idea that, even as our Higher Selves, some of us really love their All-That-Is-ness, and maybe couldn't care less if Source were infinite or not.

And then there are those of us who are more like, "No, it's so important that Source is infinite. We've got to try new things. We get bored easily, and we don't like to be bored."

That idea was so funny to me. I'd never thought about it or seen it that way, and for some reason it feels really good.

If you're feeling as if you're floating, let's do something to get you back into your body.

Stay in Your Body

Floating is fine, but I'm not a fan of out-of-body experiences, because I see energetically what that looks like and I don't like what I see. One of the major downsides to out-of-body experiences is that one feels that one's body is in the way of one's consciousness, but it isn't.

The misunderstanding creates energetic misalignment between the human system and the Higher Self, preventing the human self from more readily accessing all the yumminess that the Higher Self energy field offers us while we're here.

I do encourage you, if you're feeling floaty, to make sure that your body is with you in that process. You can just pull on your earlobe for a minute. Strum your fingers on your eyebrows on each side. Tap your nose, tap your chin, tap your sternum, tap your knees, wiggle your toes, wiggle your fingers. You don't need to stop floating; just make sure your body is part of that experience.

Thank you, everyone here who's participating in this reality, who is accessing that awesome, unique soul signature Light of God that you are, and that no one else is. No one else could be if they tried. I love your Light, and love doing everything I can to help support that Light of you in this reality, to support how you want to live your Light and how you want to live your life.

Let's start with a nice deep breath here—in through the nose and out through the mouth. Okay, now let's do a bit of visualization and a brief centering meditation.

I'd like you to imagine that in the center of your heart is a stream of Light that looks like the Sun in our solar system.

There is your own beautiful version of the Sun, within your heart space. As you imagine it, please appreciate how warm and loving it is, how life-giving that Light is.

The Sun, or, as I call him, Sol, is very reminiscent of the life-giving properties of our soulfulness. Now, imagine that your own Sun is actually creating its own atmosphere, and that this atmosphere of Light is your human energy field. There is this beautiful sphere, this beautiful ball of energy that's naturally created by the glow of your eternal essence, your God Spirit energy that you are in the All That Is.

Notice that there is a bit of an edge to that bubble. This ball of energy that is you has some distinction between yourself and others, and that actually serves us, especially in this reality. It serves us in being our Light amid whatever anyone else is choosing or not choosing to experience in this reality.

It gives us more independence, more autonomy. It gives us access to our sovereignty that's not dependent upon what anyone else is doing or not doing here. It's a wonderful system of Light that we each—all life and us—also have access to in this world. I highly encourage you to recognize the freedom, the independence, and the choices that you have within this energy field of your Light. Sol just wants to come in and add some things here.

Sol: Your Light Is Meant for You

> *These life-giving properties of the soul essence, the Sun of your own within you, can shine Light on others.*
>
> *But it's really designed for you. It's designed for you and your Higher Self to utilize this Light of you within*

this reality however you choose to. But you can't shine the Light for somebody else. Just as I, as the Sun, can't shine the Light and provide life-giving properties to other solar systems. It's just not the structure that I have, and it's also not the structure that you have.

So the very best way, in this reality of ours here, is to recognize the differentiation between what's in your control and what's not in your control. The shining of the Light on others, perhaps to help them see their own Light, is definitely an option. But it doesn't always go the way that we want it to, does it? That free will thing comes into play.

Okay, beautiful. Sol just kind of helped us turn up the volume on how that Light is streaming into us here. And we can actually pull up that Sun through the chakra system within us to help us feel it more clearly and know it more consciously. There you go.

Mary Magdalene's New Vision for Christian Churches

With your eyes open now, we're going to dive right into the next experience here. There is a union that's taking place. I've just returned from a sacred Mary Magdalene tour that a group of us experienced in France and Rome. And I wasn't sure, as human Jill, how this was going to be incorporated in this book. But there's something that Mary Magdalene is actually asking me to share with you here, from my perspective.

There was an experience in a place of worship in Saintes-Maries-de-la-Mer, which is said to be (and I believe this is true) where Mary Magdalene and her group arrived into France on the shores of the Mediterranean.

We were in a cathedral where the locals go to worship. One part of the cathedral has a beautiful Mary Magdalene painting, and when you sit down where I was in one of the pews, she appears to be looking right at you. And she started to come through energetically.

> *Jill, wouldn't it be great if, at the front of the church in Christian churches around the world, at some point it would be not just Jesus but Jesus and me, right next to him, as a true representation of the integrated divine feminine and divine masculine?*
>
> *A human male version and a human female version, together as a unified force of love incarnate, a beautiful representation and model of how the closeness of Light in our hearts can be known and felt and embodied without the games, without the separation-age shenanigans.*
>
> *Just truth in Light. Just pure divinity. And this image is actually where we're headed, so that it will not be just Jesus but both of us, together. Maybe, in those future churches, he'll even be off the cross.*

I love that vision given by Mary Magdalene for where our current situation will possibly lead. There are so many possible scenarios for our future.

I like the idea that, for those who like organized religion and find benefit in it, which is their free will in action, at some point in the future someone will say, "Did you know that there was actually a time when there was just Jesus alone at the front of these churches? And now we have both Jesus and Mary Magdalene, because we know that they're together."

Everyone will say, "Really? There was just Jesus? How did we not know about Mary Magdalene?" And then we'll have this whole story to tell about how we kind of left Mary out because she didn't fit our patriarchal version of how we once saw ourselves.

My Team and I thank you so much for this opportunity to engage with you and your human and your Higher Self energies, in this seaming together of these cycles. We are still just absolutely relishing and celebrating this experience and this chance to engage and directly participate with you in this process. It's absolutely unprecedented, and we're excited for what this may mean for humanity, going forward.

There are many ways that loving individuals can feel delayed by the many challenges that arise in this world. Some of you may actually not feel like you want to move forward into the future without knowing that everybody is okay, without feeling confident that there's a path and a plan and a chance for those who are not in an experience such as this book provides, for those who may be suffering.

Let's address this, because it is very important and it matters to us as well. It matters to all of us that you have this information and a sense of clarity.

I'm going to let Jesus come in and be the spokesperson.

Chapter Ten
Jesus: The Suffering of Others

We've already talked about the fact that things were not perfect when I was incarnate. And you have a knowing, as your Higher Self, that when being in the physical and witnessing first-hand any sort of pain, suffering, stress, anxiety—all the forms of separation that happen in this world—it's very difficult to see that, and especially for those of you who know yourselves to be empaths.

You are sensitively wired and can feel others' pain. I know this. I knew it in my journey as Jesus, and I can relate to this. Let me offer you some, perhaps, adjustments to your perspective.

This reality is highly complex and confusing in the way that it offers free will without the recognition that it's free will.

Consider how very tricky it is that someone who is in a state of agony doesn't see that they actually have many additional choices, alongside the agony.

Their Higher Self sees it, as might anyone who has a different spectrum of consciousness, some would say a "higher vibe," or those who work with energy in another way. They might see the other choices.

But often the individual in agony can only see the agony. And the constrained emotions and sensations in this reality can feel like a vice, like a grip that they can't get out of.

So, for those individuals who want to have more joy, more Light, and a lighter version of their humanness, it's necessary to do some reconfiguration of how they look at themselves as their human. How they identify themselves as their human. How they allow for that identity to include the eternal energy of their Higher Self, amid the human experience that they're having.

As you know, at this present time on Earth, very few have that information. Very few even know it's available. And that was true when I was there, too.

So what do you do?

What do you do when you know that there are other options? That there is not just one solution, but many, for relieving the pain and suffering in this world? How do you move forward without leaving anyone behind?

The way you move forward is by knowing and embodying the structure of Light that works for you.

You definitely have the option of holding yourself back to hold the hands of others, to help guide and assist. That is one hundred percent your prerogative, and because of this consternation that you have about what will happen to the others, some of you do choose to somewhat delay your expansion and delay moving forward in your spiritual experiencing of Light in human form.

For me as Jesus, I just got over that at some point. I realized that this reality was all about that experience being a possibility. I realized that the individuals' Higher Self energies were not in that pain.

This acknowledgment that I had, this realization, didn't make the agony that they were experiencing go away. And it also didn't make me indifferent to the pain that they were suffering. But it definitely changed my perspective of my choices when confronting their choices.

I actually realized, as Jesus, that it felt better for me, felt more honoring of my Light, if I allowed myself to consider that their Higher Self was getting some benefit, some sense of, "Wow, isn't Earth a crazy reality when you can have this pain and suffering together with all these other joyful, loving vibrations that are right next to it on the bookshelf? Isn't this amazing?"

When I, as Jesus, chose to count on that, something really important happened. Again, somebody else's suffering didn't go away by my looking at that. But my perspective regarding their pain and suffering changed.

It's Not Rude to Be Happy

The magic that happened is that I allowed myself to embody more of my Light. Because, for many, and I'm mainly speaking of the brains and egos, the story that you're telling yourself may be, "It's just rude of me to embody all this Light that I now realize and have access to, while I'm amid the pain and the suffering that's here. It feels unconscionable."

I honor that interpretation. There is a lot of love and a lot of logic and intelligence in that version of interpreting the facts in a story. But, sisters and brothers, I see you, and I see that this reality continues to allow for that experience of pain and suffering.

I see your ability to access Light. I see your sense of the energetic structure that you put into place, with some decades of work in many cases, to come to this understanding that you are eternally Light . . . even while you're human . . . even when you may be the one in pain and agony.

That structure allows you to embody Light in this reality, exactly as it is. I want to offer you a new version of your story, a new interpretation of the same set of facts.

The "before" version is, "It just seems rude to be so happy, shiny, and glowing amid the suffering in this world. I can't make sense of that.

"That just seems wrong. It seems insensitive. It seems unloving to be so loving, to be so Light-based, to be this glorification of Light in human form despite the present state of affairs. I can't make sense of that, I can't make that go together."

So I'm not going to ask you to change your story. I love you as the beautiful part of the human race that you are,

*and you're exactly right. You're not wired to make sense
of that. So I love you enough to not ask you to.*

Dimming Your Light Isn't Helping

*But here's what I know from my experience as Jesus.
The reason I am still talked about today is that I experi-
mented and explored. I was very curious about a way
that I could know with certainty the Light of God that I
am, even amid the suffering that was then going on in the
world and continues to go on in the world.*

*I was pretty proud of the level of Light I was able to
hold in human form.*

*And though that was all those years ago, you still have
the pain and suffering—and, in my opinion, you now have
even more. Because the population of the planet has grown,
and the percentages of pain and suffering haven't gotten that
much better . . . and have in some cases just gotten worse.*

*The gifts of media and technology are a wonderful
thing, but sometimes it isn't helpful to know the suffering
that's happening on the other side of the globe when there
is little that you can do about it.*

*Because each and every one of you is your own
structure. That allows for each and every life form to
experience its Light or to know extreme lack of Light in
any given moment—or even throughout that life journey.
This freedom to choose is imperative for the way that this
world works.*

*Dimming down your Light actually isn't helping,
either. It may make sense in the story you've been telling*

yourself, but it actually isn't making things better. The best way that I know of to make things better is to be that hope—to be the purest vision of Light in human form that you will allow yourself to be, even in the face of someone else's suffering.

Commiseration can be helpful, but not if you collapse down to their contracted state. However, when someone feels as if they're in a very dark passage, your offering hope that the Light is still here in this reality is something altogether different.

Miracles Happen, But May Not Be Received

Now, your brain may never have the evidence, the facts and figures that it wants to be able to do a scientific study on one method of being present and offering help for the suffering of another in a contracted state, relative to the other option I'm describing. That other option is that you choose, even in the face of someone's pain, to be an embodiment of God's love and God's glory as you are allowing yourself to imagine it in that moment, as you're allowing yourself to represent it in that moment.

That's where miracles happen. There are no patterns or breakthroughs of miracles from a state of contracting oneself to meet somebody else where they are. It's a quantum mismatch. A miracle cannot happen there. In order for a miracle to occur, one of the participants must be allowing, in that moment, the breakthrough of Light that is eternally loving, unconditionally honoring. You then become a vehicle for a miracle.

But here's the sad part: you have no control over whether or not they receive the miracle of that Light. The documented miracles in this reality have been a factor of the embodied sender, if you will—the holder of the Light— and someone who is able to be the recipient of that Light.

From our perspective, miracles can happen. There is the opportunity for miracle making in every breath, in every blink, in every smile, and in every tear. And the reason that they don't happen more often is because of the state of disrepair on the recipient side. Feeling contracted.

In other words, feeling flat and small and hopeless and helpless in your humanness actually repels the positive, in something like a magnetic repulsion. One is so busy and so dedicated to the spin of the separated state that one can't even notice. It's as if the miracles just kind of fly right by like a bird.

"Oh—did you see that bird"?

"What bird? I didn't see a bird. Are you sure there was a bird?"

"Yeah! It was a white dove. It flew right by you. You didn't see that?"

A Ride You Can't Get Anywhere Else

But I get it. It hurts, in the human form, to witness the repelling of Light that you are offering or that anyone else is offering. It can be heartbreaking. I'm not asking you to get over that, because I don't know if that's possible. For me, I allowed the heartbreak sensation, and I also opened myself to the acceptance that, even if my human brain can't make sense of free will in this reality and of why it's a good idea, why it was ever offered here when we make such bad choices, somehow this all works.

Because people keep coming back here. Souls keep reincarnating here, because this is a ride that you can't get anywhere else. And the contrast of the most contracted state of Light alongside the most accepting form of Light is such a paradox. It makes for strange, strange experiences.

And Gaia is just saying, "But it doesn't deny the beauty that's here."

No level of separation, no level of contraction, can snuff out the Light of God that is here. That will never work, either, and that's a good part.

So perhaps the next time that you come across one of the many forms of evidence of the pain and suffering that's here, perhaps you will notice it.

Allow yourself to feel any empathic pain or compassion for whoever is on that experiencing end. Then you can place your hand on your heart and imagine your energy field relative to their energy field.

And you can embrace the gift that, even while that other individual, that other being of any physical form, is experiencing what they're experiencing, you have the authority to shine your Light as brightly as you want to. You can feel that love, that compassion, just as your Higher Self does.

That's not jumping into their energy field and trying to save them. If their own Higher Self isn't, then why would we want to? That's actually an unfair question, because I know why we would want to. But, again, it doesn't work well.

Shine Your Light, But Don't Impose It on Others

I'm encouraging you to notice the patterns of behavior that lead to your holding back on your Light, dimming your Light because you feel as if it's a good idea. Dimming your Light isn't helping you or others. You will likely find that when you turn up your light, even when another is having a hard time in their life, it actually feels more honoring and more loving.

Share your eternal glow when it's needed most. Turn it up and get that glow on, because that doesn't have to mean that you're being insensitive, that you're being rude, that you're being unloving, that you're not being compassionate.

Perhaps it's the most loving response, and you just didn't know until you tried it. Another reason this is important is that there have been a lot of untruths and misunderstandings. A lot of myths have been offered to spiritual communities about how, if you just turn up the Light, everything is going to get better and the pain and suffering in this world will go away.

Have you noticed that you've been turning up the Light now for quite a while, and the pain and suffering are still here? And our partner, Jill, is sitting here saying, "I don't like it when we have to deliver that news. I don't even like that that's true.

I wish, in this case, that the myth were reality, because I see how brightly our Lights shine, and I wish it were the case that your Light would melt away the bad choices or the misinformation others are operating from that keeps them trapped in a state of not knowing the love of God in their heart. Of not knowing their potential, of not seeing the amazing choices that they could also be making.

At some point I realized that that just isn't how this world works. It wasn't set up that way. But let your Light shine anyway.

We can't impose our light, God's love, our expanded consciousness, onto others. They can still choose to hide from it. Earth is actually a great place where one can hide from God's eternal love. And, as far as I can see, it's not even an option for us to change that.

We tried, by the way. We tried to change that pattern; we tried to hijack others' free will and impose forced Light upon them, because it wasn't working the way we thought it should and it wasn't working the way we wanted it to.

So those of us with a higher vibrational range and a lot of amazing technology came up with a system of blasting Light, God's Light, into this reality and almost finding a loophole around individual free will. Do you know what happened? The whole thing imploded. Do you know what we call it? Atlantis.

We denied the free will of others. We dishonored, and we rationalized it so well. We really thought we were doing the right thing. So we can now, maybe for the first time ever, really understand what happened in Atlantis.

Those of us who were part of Atlantis are talking to us here, saying, "Please don't make that mistake again.

Please hear us when we share with you that this reality offers pain and suffering. And you can choose however you want to respond to that, but it doesn't have to deprive you of the infinite energies of God Source Love that are available here."

Just because there is pain and suffering here, it doesn't have to get in the way of your being your Light. Allow your Light to be, right alongside the pain and suffering that is available on Earth. Don't wait for the pain and suffering on Earth to go away so that you can then be your Light. Because you could be waiting forever. It's still a choice. And it's still chosen. Every day. That is free will. Conscious or not.

You don't have to shut off or dim your Light because of what you see in this world. You're not of this world in that way, so why act as if you are? Dimming your Light is at odds with your purpose for incarnating. You came to be your Light. Not just when things became ideal. Not because you expected everyone else to awaken. Because you can. Now. And every Now. And so it is.

Chapter Eleven
Jesus: One Mistruth about Being Your Light

What we're sharing with you here rips the lid off of Light in your human form. It can also change the trajectory of the upcoming years. Because what has, in many ways, been containing and providing something like a glass ceiling on God-based energy incarnate in this reality, is teachings exactly like the one that we have just deconstructed.

The mistruth, the lie, that in order to heal this planet, to remove all pain and suffering, you just needed to be your Light for others, kept you dependent on how others were doing. That made you feel like you were responsible for the suffering in this world.

Because, at some level of you, you knew you were the Light of God. At some level of you, you knew even as a young child that you had access to divine energy and hope and healing and alchemy and love and clarity.

You knew things that, for whatever reason, the others, probably even in your own family, didn't seem to know. You sensed that you were different, and you were right.

So, at some point, you were offered a truth that all you needed to do was be that and everything would get better. How long ago was that? That person whom you love so much who offered you that truth, or that group that you love so much who offered you that truth, are they better, or are they still choosing separation?

Let's just allow a moment here of mourning . . . because that wasn't true, because that didn't work. Even if you really wanted it to work. Even if there are parts of you that still really want it to work.

Allow yourself to be sad or angry. But that isn't how things have been going, and from our perspective it's not how they will go, either. You've been doing everything right. In other words, you've been being your Light like a rock star, like the master that you are.

It's not broken equipment on your part. It's the system, the design of this reality that honors free will. And, as we pointed out, we tried to change that, and that didn't go well, either.

Don't Be a Dictator of Light

Dishonoring free will does not go well in this reality, not even when it's well intended, not even when there's a beautifully benevolent group that wants beautiful things for all people.

If it dishonors the experience that another is having and choosing to have, whether choosing it consciously or choosing unconsciously, you're in a kind of dangerous territory. Instead of being like a usual dictator who would cause pain and suffering, you're trying to dictate Light in this world, and that doesn't go well.

There are other ways to do this in which you don't have to be a dictator of Light. You have the ability and authority and mastery to experiment with your Light in totally new ways. Any way that you want to.

And one goal that might be helpful is for when you see that person who sometimes makes you really wish you could step in there and just make a couple of adjustments, change a couple of decisions, change a couple of thought patterns and they'd be better. They'd be good as new. They'd be better than new.

We're talking about that person in your life who makes you really wish you could get in there and tinker a little bit with their wiring—for their benefit, so they could be closer to the Light of God that you know is available and that they are pushing away without even realizing it. They're turning away from it, and maybe even turning away from you.

Think of that person for a moment. One goal, one objective that you might want to consider for yourself is, "Can I stand fully in the Light and love of my Higher Self and their Higher Self and feel nothing but honor and respect for this amazing journey that they are having? While also not denying my human layers that are just sad that this person is suffering? They get so frustrated, and it seems like they keep running into that same wall over and over again."

All you want to do is just give them a hug, put your hands on their shoulders, and say, "Go this way. Every time you go that way, you get hurt. Have you noticed that?"

Some of you might even have done that. Might have said many, many times to that individual, even to that animal kingdom group that goes through pain and suffering, "No—go this way!" And then they may get it for a second, and it might seem that you were right. Yet you notice again within a short time that they're right back where they were before.

But their Higher Self is still loving and honoring them. Their Higher Self is not saying, "Oh, no, this is terrible. I've got to get them out of there." Their Higher Self is saying, "I love them so much and I don't want to see them suffer, either. Yet this is a weird reality on Earth. I'm glad I know that, as our eternal selves, we're always okay."

We're okay no matter what happens on Earth. I'm glad I know that there were many very loving, divine reasons that we created this reality—even though it includes the option for pain and suffering, even when that pain and suffering is happening to my human or my physical me in this reality.

It's Not Our Job to Fix Everything Here

I'm speaking as Jill here. When I first channeled that last bit there, my inner response was, "Easy for *you* to say, Jesus and Team, as the Higher Selves who don't have to sit there and look at it and see it."

And do you know what they said?

> *You're right. You're exactly right. It is easier for us, because we have that broader perspective of what this reality is and why it works this way and why it's allowed to exist, why it's still beautiful amid the pain and suffering, and why free will allows Source Creator God to be infinite versus static and finite and boring.*

So, in my response as Jill, I said, "Well then I want to do everything I can to offer that perspective. Because if that helps you guys be all chill and loving 'up there,' then I want to pull that in down here."

And they said,

> *Great idea, great idea, you do that.*
> *But just don't think, Jill, that it's going to remove the pain and suffering from this world, because it's only going to remove some of the pain and suffering from those who choose to hear you, who choose to make it their truth and deploy it.*

And they're right. It doesn't fix everything here. And now I can more fully appreciate how that's not our job, to fix everything here. But I know that we can each be a much more upgraded version of our love and our Light when the goal is to be the representation of God's love that is akin to the Higher Self we just described, while also having perhaps the disadvantage, but also the advantage, of having actual flesh and blood and bone.

I know what it is to be standing there right beside them, or being right there on that phone call, allowing that love of God to stream through you even while you're crying, even while you're frustrated that there's a part of you that wishes this reality didn't work this way.

Yet you're still allowing yourself to be this expanded version of love that can include all of that. That can make room in your Higher Self to be angry, to be sad, to even be depressed, while also allowing yourself to not constrict into those essences and to stay expanded, to also allow, right alongside that, that Higher Self perspective.

And Jesus just said, *That's the way I did it.*

He has much more to say on this topic of the free will of every Higher Self embodiment.

Jesus As Brother, Not Hero

That's why you're still talking about me today. Not as a hero. In this group you know me as the brother that I am, and that I will always be to bringers of Light into this reality who love, love, love, even when you're not asked to, even when somebody doesn't seem to want you to care.

You never put down that love, and you wish deep in your human heart that everyone felt that way. Because you know that they have the choice, you know that there's always hope that someone can turn things around. And you're right.

But there's also an emotionally mature acceptance that they may not yet have developed, and you have the opportunity to create a way to be okay with that, to be okay with their choices.

We sincerely hope that what we've talked about today will be instrumental in that process, or will at least help you get closer to that level of divine acceptance that is not easy—especially if you're going through the inner workings of the brain in order to get there, because it's not logical.

So don't ask it to be human logic. Ask it to be divine logic, the same divine logic that allowed this experiment to ever go forward, this amazing reality of Earth and free will, of unconsciousness amid consciousness.

This divine experiment contains a wide, wide range of levels of Light, including the most dark, for which some religions would come up with a word like "evil."

And, for the brightest Light, some would come up with the term of "God in human form." Or "saints." Or "human angels."

Know that, without an appreciation for this reality exactly as it is, you will be blocked from moving forward. Not by anyone else, but by your own beautiful brain, by your own sense of logic, your own interpretation of facts.

You might stubbornly say, "I know I'm the Light of God. I know I've got a lot of things figured out, and I refuse to move forward without everybody else moving forward with me."

You can refuse, you can. You have that free will to refuse to move forward further in your Light. You have that option.

And you also have the option of saying, "I think that isn't going to have the effect that I wanted. I understand free will better now, and I want to consider the idea that I'm not here to fix this planet—even though I really wish I could, because I love it. I love it here. I love how I know God, and I want everyone to know that Light within them. I want everyone to feel the love that I feel for them as the God energy that I am."

But most will not choose to receive. So you can stay right where you are, refusing to move forward.

But know that the reason we're even communicating for this book is to help point out all the choices you have to actually move forward, to create a system of understanding for yourself in another way—we would say an upgraded way—how Light works here and how it works in a world of free will.

Honoring the Lack of Light on Earth

You can keep going, because—again—you're really busting through that glass ceiling, just as you've done so many times. But this is a big hurdle for a lot of bringers of Light in this reality. And, for a larger group of you, doing this is unprecedented and very exciting.

This is what we've been talking about today: about honoring, if you will, the lack of Light in this reality.

Among bringers of Light across the ages, honoring the lack of Light on Earth has been a limiter for many.

You can see that. There are many signs of it, many evidences of someone operating from that mentality and structure and saying things like, "You know, when this happens, then everything is going to get better."

That's a telltale indicator that they're working from what we call that false ascension program. That idea that everybody is going to get there together, that everyone is going to wake up and see the Light if we're just shiny enough.

"But how could they deny it?" you might wonder.

I'll tell you how they can deny it. They can deny it because of the way that free will works in this reality, and they can deny it because we've tried that before, in Atlantis, and it didn't work well. It went very badly.

Empathy Can Be a Trap

There's another evidence of that false ascension program. And, yes, we're sounding judgmental, and we're okay with that. We have very strong opinions, which is why we're as clear as possible about where things will get you—where it's likely to lead, based on everything we see happening, on how this reality is structured, and on what has happened before.

Another telltale sign is when someone's saying or animating (that is, acting out) this truth of, "I will allow more of my Light in when others are receiving their Light. I don't want to go too far forward because I feel like I'm abandoning a group if I shine too much right now. It just feels like this is better. I'm going to hold off on the full glorification of my human for now, because I want to stay back and be there for them."

Another way that you can be there for them is to truly let in that infinite love, that infinite Light, right now. At least try it, brother, sister. Sometimes their receiving that miracle, that healing, is actually a higher likelihood when that Light is not so held back in you.

We know that feels strange. It feels weird to be this full-on love ball in the face of the pain and suffering right in front of you.

That is still an unconscionable way to be, even to many who have already heard this message and heard it well, because putting it into practice is a different game.

That's why we have this book. Read it as many times as you need to. Share experiences of how it worked and how you did it with others in your spiritual tribe.

Did you allow your energy to shrink in empathy, or did you keep it going forward? By the way, it's not just empaths who fall into this. We're going to be really blunt and just call it a trap.

We were showing this a lot to Jill when she was on her adventure in France. One of the other participants in the sacred Mary Magdalene group made a comment on the bus because we were going to so many sites that were originally pagan.

The pagans recognized the raw, pure divine energy that was at some of these sites, and they would build temples in these places or even build their homes on these sites, because it felt like home. Home in their hearts here on Earth.

Jill: The Pagans of France

They built these sites, and then churches came in later. The church authorities also recognized the energy, so they put a cathedral right on top of it.

It was like, "What paganism? This is the church bringing the Light here. This isn't raw energy in human form. It's the church that made this place so good."

That's funny, right? But sometimes not so funny.

While we were in France, one of the participants in the group said, "Wouldn't things possibly have been better, Jill, if we had just left the pagans alone? They had something that worked, and then the church messed it all up." (I'm paraphrasing here, but this is kind of what she was saying.)

And I, as human Jill, was feeling as if that was a good point. Then my Team said,

> *Actually, you can still go further than the pagans did. Do you know why? Because the pagans still had things on altars. Even the Greeks did, and the Romans and so forth. They still believed their underlying ideology that humanity wasn't glorified, that humans were flawed, and that certain sacred objects were holding Light better than we were.*

So the idea was that we needed to worship them. We needed to honor them in a way that dishonored ourselves. It's as if they were closer to God than we are, whether that was a stone or a certain crystal that was closer to God than we are, or nature was closer to God than we are . . .

Gaia has a wonderful belly laugh going on now. She's laughing about that form of worship: *Oh, you just said it, sister, because I have never said that before. Thank you for saying that!*

I mean, dear reader, you might have walked away from organized religion, but some of us still have some of those somewhat pagan ideas. There's nothing at all wrong with that. There is free will, and we have those choices, right?

The Team is saying,

> *We just want to make sure that you consciously under-stand what you may be doing without realizing it. We love you enough to be really, really clear—and sometimes exceedingly blunt—about how we see things.*

So whenever your beautiful brain interprets that something else is closer to God than you are, my Team and I hope you put a big old target on that and see it as a great opportunity. The pre-religion pagans had a lot of things that worked, and even organized religion actually has some things that work. (We appreciate that many of you really don't like it, for very good reasons.)

But the pagans had their own challenges, too. They had their own version of separation. For many of them, it was like, "Well, so and so may be a human version who's close to God, but I'm not that. I'm not close to God."

Meanwhile, the Higher Self might be saying,

Oh, my gosh, here I am, here's the thought pattern, here is this assumption, here is this "truth" that I'm pretending is real—the one that's keeping me from accepting the pure glory that I actually have full access to, even though I don't see it. Because that truth, that belief, that energy structure is doing its ingenious job in this human Earth reality of keeping me from feeling it, knowing it, seeing it, realizing it.

Every form of life is maybe one to three adjustments of "truths" away from a high degree of inner glorification of God within their form. Everyone.

This is interesting . . . one of the Greek gods is coming. Oh, it's Hercules. We saw statues of Hercules in Rome, but I've never heard from him before.

Chapter Twelve
Hercules: Godly Attributes

Hello, friends. There is an advantage to having some human-form representative who appears like a full-on glorification of God in whatever his or her supposed godly attributes are. To a member of humanity, it can actually be uplifting to know that at least somebody, at least some semi-human, has these godly attributes.

Then, of course, in the Greek times we made them into gods. Humans became gods; gods became human. Can you imagine such a reality, possibly even now, in this seeding and further perpetuating of a new cycle of human experience?

In this new cycle, more and more of you are realizing that all of you are God in human form.

All of you are our human-form representations who have multiple versions of yourselves and who have full

authority to be the broken version of your humanness.
The depressed version of your humanness. The full-on
godly version of your humanness. All of you. And it's
very possible that the ones you most want to inspire and
help are more likely to see that in themselves by seeing it
first in you.

It is possible, as more and more of you further allow
the glorification of yourselves, for others to respond in
any of multiple ways. And there is the possibility that
some whom you love the most will come up with stories
like, "Well, he's not really as great as he thinks he is," or
"She's arrogant."

In other words, it can seed jealousy and insecurity in
others. The self-doubt comes across as, "Well, of course,
Hercules—you were a god. But I'm just me. I'm way less
than you."

That's the insecurity being seeded. Still, that is a
choice, so that's possible. But the other possibility is that
those who know you, those human representations whom
you most care about—won't always be coming from the
human brain and human ego.

Helping Others to Feel the Light of God in Themselves

It's very possible, as you're further allowing your
full-on godliness, that exaltation of humanity, that they
will want nothing but to celebrate that.

They may respond to this glorification of your Light
in human form by exclaiming, "Oh, dear God, you're
glowing from the inside out." And, should they choose

to honor you and celebrate you, witnessing your Light in an honoring way may help them to feel the Light of God in themselves.

When they're choosing to take back more personal responsibility for their emotions and feelings and health and nutrition and finances and all the litany of things that can send a human into a tailspin, it helps them to all of a sudden have those breakthrough moments when they're not banging into that wall over and over again.

Human consciousness in this reality is a huge driver of the overall reality, and Gaia just said, "Amen." For that reason, many have chosen to demonize human conscious-ness, blaming it for the ills of this world.

Human consciousness as a collective is not like the aspen trees. It's not a community. Human consciousness is very different. Yes, you are all connected, but you have this individuality, a natural divine division from human to human to human. That gives you the authority to upgrade the grid system that's available to all of humanity. But you're not forced to do so; it's perfect.

To be human is to be at a totally different level of personal responsibility. It's a completely different journey from the other journeys for which you've chosen to be other physical forms—whether that was a tree, a plant, a mineral, or other forms of animal life. It's a whole different deal.

There is this projection that you, as your human—with your allocation, if you will, of human consciousness—are somehow responsible for the rest of human consciousness, or that what the rest of human consciousness does is a reflection of you.

I really encourage you to step out of that mind-control bubble because, again, it will keep you in a state of limitation that will block you from moving forward.

Jill here. Hercules is just smiling at me, saying, *"I can't believe you didn't say this earlier,"* and he's giving me a hug. Thank you, Hercules. He's laughing, and saying, *"Okay, let me go back and get that."* He and I are both laughing right now. Thank you! Back to Hercules.

The False Program of Human Disenfranchisement

Moving forward means the further acceptance of the pure Light of God that you are as A: your Higher Self, and B: whatever else you're knowing yourself as, including your human. This saddy-waddy sort of heavy armor of, "Oh, I'm human, so I'm broken" is no different, energetically, than the idea of original sin that many of you walked away from.

Isn't that interesting, that many of you realized that the concept of Adam and Eve and original sin was pure nonsense, and yet there are all these other ways that this reality keeps handing you back these shackles.

It's as if it's saying, "But you're human here. You're really broken, you're really disenfranchised, because you chose to be human. Good luck, good luck with that humanness."

That is a false program that's being heavily laid on some of you, and it really is up to you to realize that and slow down your thoughts so that you can really hear what you're saying to yourself in response to that program, at the deep, deep level of your ego that ends up creating your reality.

Now, the good thing is that everything we've been doing in this book project is helping to soften those inner stories that have you in a state of separation. We're softening their hard edges and helping you to see them more often. Everything we're doing is helping you to attune, inviting you into that beautiful Chamber of Light and helping you to feel more of that true divinity within you so that you can notice the contrast.

You see, that's what this one, Jill, means to me. That's what this one does best. She helps you remember what it feels like to be your God essence. Not through what she says, but through the energy that she has chosen to carry in this lifetime.

She uses a lot of words because she's chosen to be a master communicator. That's her thing; that's how she keeps you reading here for hours.

But what's really going on is that these words are containers for the energy that Jill embodies. And they are containers for the energy that we're offering, because we love you readers who have felt drawn to this book, and we wish that everyone on the planet could be reading it.

Because we actually would like it if every single form of life on the planet would all of a sudden choose love, choose to know the Light of God that they are. That wouldn't disappoint me one bit—for me to finally, even as Hercules, be able to look eye to eye, peer to peer, with my fellow humans.

Who Have You Put on a Pedestal?

They would not be exalting me as some rare form of human that they'll never be. They would be appreciating my version of divinity in human form while also appreciating their own—feeling the unique and reverent opportunity that all Higher Selves feel when they choose to incarnate.

They'd be feeling the divine honor of playing in this reality in any form that's been chosen, and the unique way that that comes through in humanity.

So here's my question to you, dear brothers and sisters. Now that we see ourselves as peers, who do you have on that pedestal?

I'm not asking you to knock anyone down. That's an immature, egoic way to make yourself feel better.

I'm just asking you to give yourself that pillar, that column, just like the ones you see all over Greece and all over Rome and in other places that have stood the test of time. Because those pedestals were manmade, they're able to represent your human energy as well as your divine energy.

Please get busy on your pedestal making. Not to put yourself up at the expense of others. But, like the statues in Rome, which are easy to see from all levels of physical life, to be the demonstration of Light that you're saying you want to be.

It can be a joyful thing to put yourself on a pedestal for the pure goal of dancing on that pedestal and saying, "I'm Light, I'm in human form. That doesn't mean I'm perfect, but I've got some things that are rock star, and you can do this, too."

I see you. Do you see you? You can be on that pedestal for the further demonstration, the further glorification of all who choose to know it for themselves. It's a pretty good way to see the world, too, when you've got your pedestal going on.

It's not about better than. (Did you hear that, ego?) We're not saying to put yourself on a pedestal in such a way as to look down on others.

Your perspective is broader when you have yourself in alignment with your God energy, and we're just using the pedestal idea as a metaphor.

When you're embracing that God energy, you see more, because even when you're having a bad day, even when in the midst of an insecurity crisis or jealousy or depression, alongside that you are also embracing your God essence.

You're also saying, "Okay, I know that part of me is a little sad today. I know that part of me is jealous about something today. But the rest of me has a lot of other stuff going on, too, and I'm going to also allow myself to know that."

That gives you a broader perspective, just as you would have if you were on a pedestal in one of those beautiful places. Make the pedestal something that you use for good—your good and the good of others.

And now Mahatma Gandhi is coming in, and he's saying, "This age of martyrdom in spirituality: please make it stop."

Gandhi: The Martyr Archetype

Thank you, Hercules. We want to give you some signs, evidences, telltale indicators, of that martyr energy. It's falsely humble. That is, it won't accept a compliment. One example is when someone offers a healing and then is quick to give all the credit to the one who allowed the healing, the one who received it, denying the facilitator role that the healer had in it.

Both the healer and the one healed played a role. It's not all one or all the other.

Another sign of a martyr, in addition to their being unwilling to accept being the glorification of God that they are in a humble, nonegoic way, is that they love to talk about how hard their road has been.

The ego feels so good when explaining the trials and tribulations of how challenging it has been to be them. "It's so hard," the martyr says, "so hard."

If this is the choice, there's nothing wrong with that. It's just a choice. But, again, the martyr archetype blocks Light, and it also sends a signal to others that they, too, have to get ahead only through sacrifice. And that's not even true.

The story of me was hijacked. My whole life journey was hijacked. And Jesus just said, "Welcome to the club." Of course we're laughing, because we both know a lot about that."

Chapter Thirteen
Practical Tips for
Being Your Light

Jill here again. Wow! We have covered a lot. I'm saying thank you to all of our Teams, for all of the beautiful energies that came through.

Together everyone here (including you) created quite a magnificent cornucopia of experience . . . together. I view you as much more than a passive reader.

I see your mastery, and I'm so excited for whatever you choose to have this mean. For me, considering our own mastery means choosing to celebrate our humanity, our having chosen as souls to be here, each of us.

In many ways, you made you.

Being Human and Divine

This approach to life offers a newfound appreciation that everyone here is both human and divine, all at the same time.

Through my own divine connection. I've realized that we don't need to battle between those two. From within our human experience we can access both, even simultaneously.

To offer more clarity, your humanness isn't getting in the way of your brilliance. Rather, your humanness was an intentionally chosen opportunity for further expressing your divinity, within human form. Your human form.

Additionally, your expressing that brilliance, in your own unique ways, does not require human perfection. Your soul understands full well the challenges and stressors of being on Earth, and isn't bothered or angered by your not being your best self in any moment.

Your soul appreciates that your humanity is happening right alongside your divinity. You can think of it as similar to the Sun always being in its place, even on a cloudy day.

Now, your soul does, of course, see the many missed opportunities for handling yourself or situations better than maybe you did. But the soul isn't angry about that, although possibly disappointed. It is always cheering for you to be a version of yourself that *you* like, enjoy, and love.

For anyone here who has experienced Christianity, we've been offered over and over again assurances of how perfect Jesus was as his human.

But I had been encountering endless clients clearly trying to be perfect and being unnecessarily hard on themselves. So I asked Jesus about whether we need to be perfect like him.

I felt him coming over to me with a smile on his face, seemingly excited about clearing something up.

He asked me if I remembered the story about him getting furious at the temple, throwing tables up and over. He was laughing lovingly at himself in recalling those experiences, and he shared that he'd had a fiery temper. He also shared that he could be quite impatient.

I said to him, "So you weren't perfect?"

Smiling, he said, *No.*

Buddha suddenly showed up in the background of our conversation, to say, *Me, neither.*

I said to both of them, "So we don't have to be perfect to be amazing, to be divine, to fully be our Light in every moment, to be ascended?"

In unison, they both responded, *Exactly.*

Then I pondered with them about why so many beautifully goodhearted individuals are trying so hard to be perfect. We concluded that they probably think they have to be perfect in order to be their best self, in order to know the divine within themselves, and to then accept the love, praise, and acceptance that God has for them.

But God already loves us, praises us, and accepts us. Even when we're being a complete jerk. Even if we're overturning tables. God understands that, while we're wearing the human bodysuit, we're in a strange, expanded range of possibilities— from divine brilliance all the way down (vibrationally) to utterly disgusting humanity.

And, yes, free will combined with disconnection from God and from our inherent goodness has seemed to have led the human race to create further and further experiences at that disgusting end of the scale.

Hell on Earth

To me that's sad, because I know we can each do better and be better. It does seem like a waste. And I am so relieved to know that God is loving and compassionate and forgiving of any ugliness that may present in any of us while we're here, whether that horridness is minor or major.

In this regard, I feel the Christians got it right: God is forgiving. But it is not just to those who accept Jesus Christ as their Savior.

Hell is something any of us humans here on the planet can give rise to for ourselves. We are that powerful and that creative, and we can be so twisted in our values that we unconsciously create our own hell to live in.

I suggest that the option of a living hell on Earth is a direct outcome of identifying oneself as an original sinner who is not inherently good and is eternally judged by a force outside of oneself that one can only pray to please and appease.

After all, what kind of life can one expect after having been told from a very young age that 1) we are born a sinner, 2) Jesus was perfect but we will never be, 3) God is an angry God, and 4) if we don't give our life to a force that's better than our sinning self, then we're nothing and God will send us to an eternal hell.

That's not exactly encouraging. It doesn't exactly inspire one to create a life of one's best self, to offer positive moral and ethical experiences for self and for others encountered in one's life.

So there is no hell after here for us to be condemned to? No. That's a story.

The reality is that hell is something created every day by humans who would probably make different choices if they gave themselves credit for their true identity as being inherently divine while also fully human.

We all have so many choices for who and what we can be, every day. It is clear to me that we make better choices when we identify ourselves as 1) unconditionally loved by God (or, in the case of atheists, at least inherently good), 2) capable of change, 3) a quite powerful creator who in so many ways *made* the life we are presently living, and 4) *capable of change* (repeated for emphasis due to its importance).

We aren't told these truths, or at least most of us aren't. So we diagnose society's problems through the lens of a growing accumulation of victimized unfairness. And that perceived injustice must be balanced out through legislation, and by others working around everyone's disenfranchised situations.

That approach plants further seeds of incapability, separation from one's creative power, and the apparent lack of inherent divinity. I appreciate the good intentions, but I see that it isn't working, and is in my view actually making things much worse.

The first place we go to when things aren't going well should ideally be, "What can I do about this to create the life I want to live?" (emphasizing personal empowerment and individual sovereignty), rather than, "Who or what can I blame for this?"

That knee-jerk tendency to blame can be replaced by the personal responsibility we can each recognize and accept. We can then extricate ourselves from the inventory of unfortunate situations on Earth that we're no longer choosing.

The power to create a life is imperative to anyone's ability to create (and then be) their best self. We cannot control everything that happens to us, no matter how positive our thoughts are. So it's important to recognize our access, always, to a hero version of ourselves—no matter what is happening or not happening.

And when you *don't* choose hero or heroine you, your soul is wanting to give you a hug and encouraging you to try again next time, loving you no matter what.

The divinity is always there . . . no matter what we, individually as humans, are choosing or not choosing. What any human does with this opportunity for being amazing and glorious is primarily a result of free will, applied will, information, and personal expectation. Personal expectation is a huge factor.

In my view, organized religions do a huge disservice in this regard. Where does it leave someone when their self-concept is that they're a naturally sinful being who will never amount to anything of value apart from their abidance to a God who is outside of themselves?

I don't view the religions' intentions as malicious as much as they are misguided. I believe they're wrong, and that turning toward one's own inherent goodness, and maximizing that, is a more certain way for us to move forward into levels of advancement, personally and also collectively.

I find that most of my audience has a knowing within themselves that they are special, important, and loved. Many left organized religions because of that mismatch of core identity (original sin vs. original divinity).

They were searching for other beings who felt the same way, and were choosing to believe in themselves and to think for themselves.

I find that I especially love supporting these individuals, for I feel a kinship with them. I am also confident that anyone can transform their life with these truths.

Anyone could find themself here, reading this and questioning the core narrative of their life, only to find that the hope they were seeking is hope in themself, in what makes them naturally good, inherently divine, and eternally loved.

In my beliefs and experience, these are the ingredients for positive transformation. Because, just as we can make for ourselves a hell on Earth, we also have the power to make for ourselves a heaven on Earth.

We don't even need to fix the world in the process. We can create a personal heaven on Earth while allowing the world to be exactly as it is, right now.

Facts of This Reality

Earth is strange, and beautiful and unpredictable. Not even God knows what will happen next. There is a loose script that we each have with every life. As our soul, we select parents, birthplace, birth time. We have some expectations based on these choices (of race, culture, community, time period, economic stratum, etc.).

As our soul, we can also insert some "pre-wiring" for that lifetime in terms of passions, interests, temperament, personality, some key strengths and abilities, and some key weaknesses and preplanned struggles.

The soul makes these choices based on a wide variety of factors, none of which are preplanned for suffering. As an example, if someone is born to abusive parents, the soul has not chosen this as a punishment, karmic retribution, or to teach the soul a lesson.

Why, then, *would* a soul pick parents for its human who have a tendency to abuse their child? This part may be harder to imagine, but the soul is aware that, no matter what happens on Earth, it, as the eternal soul, will always be okay—even splendid.

Yes, the soul is always okay. From within the Earth experience, often all that we can relate to is ourselves as humans, and we can often feel very *not* okay. There's a wide and even growing variety of horrible experiences that can happen to us on Earth. If the soul's intention were to avoid all pain and suffering, it would never choose Earth as an incarnation place.

Yet, no matter what happens to us here on Earth, the soul is fine. The soul knows this in the planning it does for each human experience it creates. The soul continues on, in its eternal blissful state, while a part of itself is having a human experience of Earth (or an animal experience, or a plant experience, etc.).

The human or other life form will suffer, in some ways, at some points, and that is a certainty. That doesn't mean that the soul is pleased with this suffering. But it knows that certain ordeals come with the territory of being on Earth.

So why would it choose incarnations here? Because Earth is uniquely amazing.

The preplanning, combined with free will, makes for an absolutely wild ride that can be marked by celebrations and also by sadness, for the soul is aware of all potential aspects of its human's journey. Yet, with every journey there is the hope that a human will transcend Earth's intrinsic difficulties. And with every journey it may not go this way.

After a particularly painful journey, it's shown to me that the soul is always ready to offer a huge hug of welcome and loving comfort following the human's mortal transition, perhaps with the communication of *I'm here; that was a hard one. It's over now. You're okay . . . we're okay.*

Based on Eastern spiritual teachings, one may be asking, "But doesn't human suffering result from karmic ties and corrections from past lives?" You have sufficient Creator energy and free will to create a life within this lens. But that doesn't make it true. If that system works for you in making sense of this reality, being your best person, and supporting others in the same, great.

For me, what I am shown is that this doesn't make sense, and actually prevents us from being our best self. Why? Because we then personalize every pain, every misfortune, every moment of suffering, into something we must have deserved.

As my Team offered it to me, *Don't confuse your experience with your identity.* On Earth we can suffer, and everyone does at some time, in some way; some more than others. But this suffering is not the purpose of incarnation, and is not our atonement for any "past life" misdeeds.

Karma and "Past Lives"

Besides, no life is "past," for the soul functions beyond the time-space continuum, where there is no time (or all time coexists) and there is no "there."

Karma and "past life" concepts are by their very nature a creation of belief that was set in motion from within this reality, just as were organized religions. If they work to help humans be their best selves, that's awesome; I have no desire to tear off a Band-Aid to expose a lie.

But, in application, even supposedly high-vibe concepts such as karma and linear past lives actually deprive one of experiencing one's own greatness. How? Because those within this belief system, if they're wanting to move forward in this life, are consistently assessing where they are in their life-ascension pathway and whether they're doing their best.

Most people whom I've experienced who live within these thought systems have no expectation of pure divinity being accessed within their own self; they seem to confer that degree of greatness only upon their gurus, masters, and "teachers."

Their sense of what's possible for themselves is anchored to a less-than-divine sense of who and what they are as a soul. They view their soul as a yet-to-be-enlightened energy field that's dependent on their doing their best in order to move forward on a linear, evolutionary pathway.

Meanwhile, their soul, which is already fully divine and fully evolved, is appreciating the free will that's involved in all of this, knowing full well that all followers of such gurus are themselves capable of pure glory and beautiful ascension experiences beyond any possible human limitations.

I asked my Team why the gurus don't tell this to their followers and students. I was then reminded that the gurus and masters don't know it, for they are also within the limited teachings, themselves.

136

Their pre-wiring, combined with believing in themselves, offered them the opportunity to know themselves as more spiritually enlightened beings. The karma and past-life model of belief placed them within the guru role. Until such masters transcend their own teachings, they will never assist their students and followers in realizing their own inherent divinity and sovereignty.

As I realized this trapped model and the students' stated devotion to divinity, love, and light, I became frustrated. I wanted them to know the truth. Not so that they would fire their guru, but so that they and their soul could have the energetic reunion that allows for that heaven on Earth experience that I know.

I want that for everyone who wants it. If the supposed masters and gurus on Earth aren't teaching this because they don't know it, then I'm happy to fill in that void. But, since I refuse to call myself a guru and don't play into the "I'm holier ·than you are" model that so many students seem to like, I might not assist as many as I could because I'm less likely to be viewed as exalted.

My truth is that we are all fully evolved (but not finite) souls who happen to also be having a human experience. It is a strange conundrum. I'm regularly amazed at what my fellow masters, who choose to act and function as gurus, choose to do with their abilities.

And I'm regularly pissed off at how they use it to separate themselves from their audience vs. draw them closer and point out their followers' own divinity.

A tip here for any of you who may identify yourself as the spiritual student of so and so: Are the teachings leaving you amazed at what your teacher can do (their mastery), or amazed at you and *your* mastery?

My preferred approach to using my mastery here is to help you appreciate your inherent mastery, your essential goodness, your eternal divinity. Because what you think of me and my connection to God is less important than what you think of yourself and *your* inherent connection to God.

Knowledge of your eternal connection to God is what's necessary for you to believe in your greatness, your glory, and your ability to transcend the limitations we all face in this world.

Also, I don't like to see intermediaries between anyone and God. Jesus just said, *Me neither.*

Our Lives Only Seem to Happen in a Series

But aren't we here to learn lessons? Isn't Earth a school that we come to as souls to learn and evolve? The idea of evolution in terms of a series of lives in which a soul learns more and more, ascending closer to God with each lifetime, has a big problem: it's stuck in a structure of linear time.

Remember how my Team and I earlier shared that the true soul is beyond the time-space conventions? At the soul level there is no before or after, as everything is happening at once.

Therefore, this notion of consecutive lifetimes building upon each other is one that was created within this reality, not at the soul level.

Does that mean that the supposed series of lives is a lie? Well, in a sense, yes, but I don't view it as a malicious one.

Buddha offers here that many an enlightened individual has offered his or her perceptions of what this Earth reality is, and those have in some cases become theology, doctrine. That doesn't mean they're true.

But, as humans, we are powerful enough in our free will to act as if it's true, thus helping to make it very real for anyone else living amid these beliefs. The soul simply views this as part of its human's free will and "chosen" experience.

But is it chosen if the individual didn't know the other choices, or even that it was a choice? That is debatable, for certain.

Here is how my Team explained choices to me: There are choices that we make consciously and choices that we make unconsciously, with a very wide spectrum along these variables. Choices for being incarnated are made at the soul level, consciously.

Everything at the soul level is done consciously, which doesn't mean the soul knows how choices going to turn out (Earth is unpredictable, and often random).

And, at the human level, those who are enlightened (acknowledging the eternal goodness within themselves) tend to make more choices from consciousness, and with conscience.

However, those who are not enlightened (not yet knowing themselves as inherently good and capable of being good and doing good) are much more likely to operate in most moments unconsciously.

Thus they make choices and decisions without much thought, consideration, or prior assessment of the potential consequences.

The power here comes in our ability to question, to be curious about even things like doctrine. Some are more inclined to question, to challenge, and to be curious. Some are less so. And there is that pre-wiring again.

So then, what is good? Good here on Earth can be relative to individual assessment, based on values, beliefs, and morals. But, in general, good can be defined as deeds and actions that are positive, blessed, and pleasing to the self and that have no intended harmful consequences to another.

Is the Soul the Same As God?

Because there is so much individuality and uniqueness to each soul, the soul is often the easiest eternal connection concept for us as humans. God, in my experience and as it is shown to me, is the widest-level concept of all souls and all possibilities. But this God concept can feel less personal, less accessible to most humans who are trying to access their own enlightenment (Light within).

How is it possible that God can't predict the future? Isn't God all-knowing? Being all-knowing or omniscient would infer that everything has already happened.

But it hasn't. (Stay with me here, because your mind may soon feel, again, as if it's being twisted like a pretzel.) That sensation is your human consciousness stretching to new levels, new ranges where it hadn't been before.

If God knew everything that was about to happen, that would mean that everything has already happened and that God is finite. But God is infinite (for my atheist or agnostic readers, you can replace the word *God* with *consciousness* here and it still works).

How is God infinite? God is infinite because God is curious. I recognize that here I could be accused of anthropomorphic reasoning, and I accept this. God is curious, as in it doesn't know how everything is going to go, and *wants* to know what is possible.

Earth (and sentient life everywhere) was created as an experiment, based on curiosity concerning what would happen if God didn't know it was God. As we've learned, when we as humans are forgetting we're God, we can do some really, really stupid things. And, we can also do some really, really beautiful things.

We don't know which way we're going to end up. Even as our souls, we don't know. But the possibilities are wide, and include the good, and the soul's divinity is intact either way, so we create human lives. And in all of our experiences here as souls in human bodysuits on Earth, we play a valuable role in God being infinite.

Is it true that God has human journeys to get to know itself? This is perhaps my favorite misunderstanding. The idea that any soul would come to Earth, with all of its free will, forgetfulness, and unconsciousness, to get to know itself is quite humorous.

Earth would be a horrible place to use for getting to know oneself. Additionally, God isn't having an identity crisis, although the human might be.

Earth is a place filled with randomness, twisted logic, unpredictability, and an almost terrifyingly wide spectrum of consciousness. A soul engages in human experiences knowing that it is most likely going to forget everything it knows as a soul.

Even souls who pre-wire their human for amazing enlightenment abilities can watch that human forget for the whole journey, only to eventually die and then report, *I forgot. Everything. Again.* [Smiling.] *Dammit! Earth is quite a ride!* And the soul also smiles.

Isn't a human journey an elaborate, dreamlike hallucination to the soul? No. This one bothers me a lot, for some reason. Part of my intense irritation with this misunderstanding is that I notice how those who believe it seem to feel very little personal connection to their human life, or to anyone else's.

If our human lives didn't matter (pun), the soul wouldn't create them. Souls create their human lives with sometimes tremendous prior planning. But, by the way, in contrast, some souls incarnate with a very loosely defined sense of just being curious to see what will happen.

Other souls incarnate with quite specific intentions; for example, to restore various divine grid systems and do so from within the human structure. Even with this pre-planning, their human can go rogue amid the forgetting and the free will and the cornucopia of options available on Earth for determining who and what one is.

So even the soul must yield in many ways to the free will of the human individual, even when that individual is their own. You are not a puppet on a string. You're a conscious being, creating your own reality based on your sense of who and what you are and why you're here.

Choosing Your Purpose

A purpose isn't so much discovered as created. Rather than ask someone like me what your purpose is, I encourage you to upgrade your own enlightenment, decide for yourself what you want your purpose to be, and live accordingly.

Choosing your purpose, now that is an upgrade. I love being a part of upgrades . . . trusting free will, that inherent goodness, and the amazing Creator power of the human spirit to do amazing things while we're here.

Jesus, Galileo, Da Vinci, Tesla, Mme. Curie, Steve Jobs, and so many others all believed in themselves. They all took themselves seriously enough to question their present-day narrative and go farther. And go farther they did.

I love imagining what every human is possible of being and contributing—for their own enjoyment and for the betterment of humankind as a whole.

Although it doesn't always go as planned, souls do indeed have intentions to upgrade the human race through their own human experience and what that offers.

And it's very strange for any of us relating to this sense of personal relevance to be alongside other humans who seem so indifferent about their own human journey (no plans, little ambition, in general fairly carefree).

It's as if these beings are here on vacation, just here to chill and forget that they are God. See what we mean?

But you heard that everyone has incarnated right now to "ascend" and become enlightened? Nope. Not true. And what a messed-up plan that would be.

Trying to get all humans to do *anything* together is a failure waiting to happen, given the free will, the wide spectrum of consciousness available, and the consistently distracting experiences here.

So no one needs to remember that they're God? Right, no one needs to remember, as Earth is a reality built for forgetting. Then why are we remembering? Because we are so unique, yes, but there is even more to it.

Some of us, as our souls, have seen the benefits of holding space for the enlightened ends of the consciousness spectrum. That isn't held in place by anything other than the humans. Jesus held space for that end of human enlightenment, as did others. It could be viewed as their reason for incarnating.

And there are times when we, as souls, want to do more than hold space for the enlightened end of human consciousness; we actually want to increase the consciousness held within humanity.

To me, that is very much a group like you, the reader, and me (you get to decide whether this is you or not).

Beings like me and possibly you can be relentless in looking for anything and everything that is getting in the way of personal sovereignty. For me this also includes regular devotion to publicly stating quite unpopular things for the purpose of increasing choice and consciousness here in this reality. Even when it comes with a personal sacrifice of individual credibility.

Is Satan Real?

Is Satan real? If you mean is there a force that is opposing God in the eternal realms, then no, Satan is not real. However, in this Earth reality, there is very much a force that can feel like it is opposing your goodness. It isn't a fair fight, as that force can quite easily be defeated through enlightenment.

I call this seemingly opposing force that we face on Earth *Wetiko*—a Cree term (Windigo or Wintiko in other Native American tribes) that refers to an evil spirit.

Wetiko is a random, disembodied, and highly opportunistic force of unconsciousness (alive but unenlightened) that can sort of impersonally take over certain individuals at any time and that operates freely within the Earthly realms.

We could say that Wetiko is at the root of every suicide, every drug addiction, every act of intentional harm done to another, every bit of twisted logic in the thinking of someone like a pedophile or sex trafficker. Is it anti-Light? No. It just doesn't know Light, doesn't operate within Light, and thrives because of lack of Light.

Then how isn't it anti-Light? When you enter a dark room in your residence, before you've turned on the light, is there a force of darkness or just a lack of light? The dark room isn't dark because of a dark force, it's dark because there is a lack of light. Turning on the light switch removes the darkness. And that is also true for Wetiko.

By recognizing one's inherent goodness, or at least option for goodness, in a given moment, one is much better equipped to face any odd urges or inner voices prompting one to do harm to oneself or others.

Wetiko thrives in situations where someone is feeling unloved, unworthy of goodness, and incapable of greatness.

In certain moments, such a person is highly vulnerable to the whims of Wetiko.

At those moments when a typically bright, aware individual says or does regrettable things, and it feels like something took them over, that is Wetiko. I can tell you that it is so freaky when it's happening. It's as if something has taken over your mouth and your body and you're in the background, watching help-lessly while the takeover is occurring. When one is enlightened this happens much less, but it does happen.

When it does, my best advice is to readily accept that you were a part of what happened, even if it didn't happen consciously. Pretending it didn't happen isn't helping anyone.

By the way, narcissists are a classic case of regular Wetiko takeovers, and their sense of importance doesn't allow them to even see their undesirable layers of self. Hence, in their energetic patterns, they have no equipment for accepting responsibility when they act like a complete a-hole.

For my fellow healers, I'm sorry to break it to you but you aren't going to be able to fix them. They must fix themselves, and that can only happen with their willingness to see them-selves and then accept responsibility for all the failings of their character.

Okay, for those here who aren't narcissists but do clearly have instances of being taken over by Wetiko, please love yourself enough to see everything you did, even when you weren't consciously doing it.

Say you're sorry to anyone you may have harmed. Tell them how you really feel about them, and ask for their forgiveness at your "losing it" for a moment there. Until you can take

responsibility for your actions, even the unconscious o
can't move forward as a whole and complete, consciou
field desiring good for yourself and others.

The upgrading mantra, if this helps, would be something like: "I am good. And, here in this instance, I messed up. I want to do better next time. I forgive myself. Earth is hard. But I can do better. I am good, and good does better."

If you're a parent, you may wonder if you'll reduce your credibility with your children by accepting responsibility for your poor behavior. Please reread that statement, possibly twice. Doesn't it make sense, even to young humans, that we only gain in credibility by taking personal responsibility and asking for forgiveness when we mess up?

Yes—we increase our credibility with others (children, co-workers, partners, friends, anyone) by sincerely admitting it when we've messed up, and asking for forgiveness. Save the rationalizations and justifications for journaling, therapy, or self-talk.

We are best able to remain conscious and avoid Wetiko takeovers by:

- having a self-identity of being inherently good but capable of big mistakes
- regularly sharing our best aspects of self with others and this world
- knowing ourselves as worthy and always capable of being absolutely amazing and eternally valuable
- showing love to ourselves through fresh air, high-quality food, loving thoughts about ourselves, and unfiltered sunlight exposure in healthy doses

147

It doesn't even take all of these things to be less susceptible to Wetiko. Even just some of these can make a huge difference. But, as long as you are on Earth, Wetiko takeovers can happen.

Jesus, on a better day of him being his best self, wouldn't have overturned the tables. He was a bit tired and more easily annoyed in that moment, and he allowed his anger to flare through his actions.

Was it okay? It was justified, yes. Does he wish he had handled it better? Yes. And, yet, it's perfect that we have this example for all of us, yes? Smile.

Thank You

Dear reader, I appreciate you. This may have been an unusual book for you to experience. You may find yourself going back to reread certain sections over and over again.

If you find yourself wanting to understand it but tuning out mentally, please just take some deep breaths, with your hand on your heart, while inviting your brain to relax and open to a completely different approach to looking at yourself and everything else.

The ego (the storyteller) can feel threatened by completely new truths. And yet, if the new story is indeed an upgrade that is allowing more of your soul into your human experience, then it's worth some temporary discomfort.

I invite you to return to that place in your heart, and I encourage you to put a smile on your face and just possibly let yourself feel excitement about the idea that some of us are not here to fit in. And that doesn't mean that we say "I'm not here to fit in" in a sad way!

It was with huge hearts and tremendous enthusiasm that our souls chose to incarnate at this time, amid everything currently going on. We knew this, and we said with hope and love and joy and divine intelligence, "I'm going to go to Earth and I'm not going to fit in there."

Some of us are not fitting in, dear readers, in all the right ways. I love you. I honor you. I'm so delighted at having had the opportunity to get to share with you.

I see your Light, I see your mastery, and I'm so glad that you, in reading this book, are here, too—not fitting in, but standing out, possibly on a pedestal across the piazza from Hercules. Possibly on a grand stage, a beautiful platform of Light that you set up for yourself in order to stand a little taller and feel a little stronger in the human form you're wearing and in the eternal Light of God that you also are. And so it is.

We allowed a lot to come through in this book. I hope you've found it wonderfully satisfying, motivating, healing, and whatever else you wanted it to be. I love to create new experiences and go at things in a new way.

There's a timelessness to what we've done here. Thank you for being a part of that. Timeless Light, here, now.

92316237R00094

Made in the USA
Middletown, DE
07 October 2018